The world spends a fortune on the means to co **[illegible]**
little on preventing conflict in the first place, or **[illegible]**
or on breaking the cycle of violence through re **[illegible]**
the use of force is sometimes the only way to **[illegible]**
*the reality is that peacemaking is much more than the conduct of military oper-
ations. As a former Royal Air Force officer, Peter Dixon lays out an enormously
helpful analysis of the issues involved. If war is far too important to be left to the
Generals, then reconciliation is far too important to be left to the politicians and
the secular world. As you read, be prepared to have your pre-conceptions about
war, peace and reconciliation challenged, but then be encouraged to engage more
deeply and effectively in a world that desperately needs to hear about better ways
of resolving conflict and about reconciliation.*

Major General (Retired) Tim Cross CBE

*Peter Dixon draws upon his considerable experience both in the military and in
his work for conflict resolution and reconciliation around the world to produce a
most compelling book. In it he delivers a focused analysis of the theories, precedent
and implications involved in both military and non-military intervention in mod-
ern-day conflicts. He offers a lucid and considered examination of the Just War
tradition as the basis to his candid appraisal of the success of conflict prevention
and peace-building through non-military means. From this he sets out an unam-
biguous, balanced and thoughtful approach, which is not to judge, but to give
pause for thought – an approach founded on a strong Christian ethos. As a work
of extraordinary relevance in today's troubled and volatile times, I commend his
book which stands out for its superb clarity and towering integrity.*

General Sir Richard Dannatt KCB CBE MC ADC, former Chief of the
General Staff (head of the British Army)

A question often asked when discussing issues of war and peace is: 'What should we actually do?' Peter's book addresses this head-on and provides helpful insights based not only on his personal experience of grappling with these issues as a professional with the Royal Air Force but also as a Christian. His biblical treatment of the subject acts as a gentle, wise and helpful companion, as we try to make sense of the conflicts in our world. His book offers us hope, never making us feel guilty, and provides a Christian framework to help us unpack complex issues as we reflect on uncomfortable questions.

Ram Gidoomal CBE
Chairman, South Asian Concern. Convenor/Chairman
'Healing the Wounds' and '7/7 and Beyond – a British South Asian
Response' conferences

An experienced Christian practitioner in the field of peacemaking, Peter Dixon has written a thought-provoking and engaging book that addresses issues surrounding war and peace in the twenty-first century. Peacemakers begins with a fresh examination of the relevance of the Just War criteria, goes on to discuss non-military intervention, and ends with an appraisal of the key area of reconciliation. He encourages Christians to engage in peacemaking, with a reminder that the Christian faith has the theme of reconciliation at its very heart. I commend this wide-ranging work which is well grounded in the practical experience of Concordis International in Sudan.

Air Commodore Mark Leakey RAF (Retired)
Director Armed Forces' Christian Union

Peace involves more than an absence of conflict at a particular moment in time. Relationships, whether interpersonal, interethnic or international, are built slowly and destroyed quickly. Peter Dixon explains how trust can be re-established, confidence rekindled and understanding restored. Given the importance of peace in Christian priorities, I hope this book will be given the attention it deserves.

Michael Schluter CBE, Founder, Jubilee Centre and Chief Executive,
Relationships Global

The London Lectures in Contemporary Christianity

This is an annual series of lectures founded in 1974 to promote Christian thought about contemporary issues. Their aim is to expound an aspect of historical biblical Christianity and to relate it to a contemporary issue in the church in the world. They seek to be scholarly in content, yet popular enough in appeal and style to attract the educated public; and to present each topic in such a way as to be of interest to the widest possible audience as well as to the Christian public.

Previous Lectures:

1997 'Matters of Life and Death: Contemporary medical dilemmas in the light of the Christian faith', *Professor John Wyatt* (published by IVP in 1998 as *Matters of Life and Death: Today's healthcare dilemmas in the light of the Christian faith*, and in 2009 as *Matters of Life and Death: Human dilemmas in the light of the Christian faith*)

1998 'Endless Conflict or Empty Tolerance: The Christian response to a multi-faith world', *Dr Vinoth Ramachandra* (published by IVP in 1999 as *Faiths in Conflict: Christian integrity in a multicultural world*)

1999 'Justice That Restores', *Charles Colson* [lectures not delivered, but published by IVP as *Justice that Restores*])

2000 'The Incomparable Christ: Celebrating his millennial birth', *John Stott* (published in 2001 by IVP as *The Incomparable Christ*)

2001 'Moral Leadership', *Bishop James Jones* (published by IVP in 2002 as *The Moral Leader: For the church and the world*)

2002 'Moving Genes: Evolving promise or un-natural selection?' *John Bryant* (published by IVP in 2004 as *Life in our Hands: A Christian perspective on genetics and cloning*)

2003 'Can Christianity and Islam Co-exist in the 21st Century?' *Professor Peter G. Riddell* (published by IVP in 2004 as *Christians and Muslims: Pressures and potential in a post-9/11 world*)

2004 'Spirituality, Christianity and the Future of the World', *Dr John Drane*

2005 'Disciples and Citizens', *Bishop Graham Cray* (published by IVP in 2007 as *Disciples and Citizens: A vision for distinctive living*)

2006 'Redeeming Family' *Revd Andrew and Revd Lis Goddard*

2007 'Redeeming Creation', *Peter Harris and Revd Dr Chris Wright*

The London Lectures Trust

The London Lectures in Contemporary Christianity are organized by the London Lectures Trust, which was established as a charity in 1994. The committee represents several different evangelical organizations.

PEACEMAKERS

PETER DIXON

PEACEMAKERS

Building stability in a complex world

The London Lectures in Contemporary Christianity

INTER-VARSITY PRESS
Norton Street, Nottingham NG7 3HR, England
Email: ivp@ivpbooks.com
Website: www.ivpbooks.com

First published 2009

British Library Cataloguing in Publication Data
A catalogue record for this book is available from the British Library.

ISBN 978–1–84474–402–2

Set in Monotype Dante 12/15pt
Typeset in Great Britain by Servis Filmsetting Ltd, Stockport, Cheshire
Printed and bound in Great Britain by Ashford Colour Press Ltd, Gosport, Hampshire

For Ingrid, Matthew and Gabriela, and for future generations

CONTENTS

FOREWORD

The first decade of the twenty-first century has stubbornly refused to live up to the hope and promise that we humans wishfully invest in the future. One could be forgiven for caricaturing the decade as a final tour of some colonial rock band, where our wayward past comes back to haunt us.

Previous tours of the Helmand River Valley in the late nineteenth century are re-enacted by the descendants of the same British regiments and tribal warriors with the same tragic consequences. Mesopotamia circa 1920s is revisited in all its complexity as a new generation adds its blood to the sands of Basra.

This generation is as burdened by the wounds of history and as haunted by its ancestral voices as any that has gone before. Nowhere is this more evident than in the ongoing drama of picking up the pieces of the collapse of the European and Ottoman Empires, which dominates the geopolitics of the twentieth century.

Ninety years after the beginning of the end of this imperial age in the fields of the Somme and the cliffs of Gallipoli, the conflicts of today are still shaped by its terrible legacy: arbitrary boundaries, ethnic divisions manipulated to maintain power, the plundering of a region's natural resources and the lingering humiliation of whole peoples. Such an inheritance continues to enrage those who wage war from the ethnic strife of the Great Lakes of Africa to the terror visited on the streets of London.

War is the constant background noise we confront only when this 'binge' violence is forced on us through its worst atrocities. Yet its effect in shaping our culture and the role of faith in our society is huge. The religiously sanctioned horror experienced by the Great War generation, the war to end all wars, is the death knell of any lingering pretence of a 'Christian' Europe, which has now worked itself out through every aspect of life in Britain.

Growing up and living in a community at war with itself in Northern Ireland, I am deeply conscious of the urgency of Christian faith in the context of war. Responding to the brutality and random suffering of violence and discerning the practical outworking of our Christian identity as peacemakers was core to the church's witness. Yet it was those outside the evangelical tradition in which I was raised who often provided the radical biblical solutions.

Within our tradition, reconciliation was too often presented as one-dimensional. Its focus was what happened in church, not what one did on the streets. In this, we were not unique in the evangelical world. What we did have was the glaring contradiction that some of those who claimed to follow Jesus best appeared to foster hate the most.

The perennial evangelical debates about the relationship between evangelism and social action, the exclusive stress on gospel and not kingdom, as much as any failure to develop a mature political and peace theology, represent an abandonment of fundamental human angst. What does faith say and what should people of faith do in the face of unspeakable terror and brutality? We are not good at addressing the affront to humanity of war, the dynamics of political power, the complexity of conflict, or the long-term process of social and cultural change over against instant conversion, which are the real challenges of our time.

Therefore, the invitation to Peter Dixon to address the theme of war and peace by those who organize the London Lectures and now this book by IVP are to be warmly welcomed. In this series of reflections, Peter does not shirk from war as a brutal episode in human relations. Protecting the weak and upholding justice appears to remain an impossible task in this violent world, without resort to violence. Peter sets out a thoughtful case, informed by experience, and then helps explore a Christian mind on conflict that highlights the practical processes of what it means to be peacemakers on the ground and amongst those who make things happen in societies.

The goal of Christian peacemaking is reconciliation. It is a word that needs rescuing, both from those who ignore the spiritual dimension and from those who see nothing else. The fundamental alienation of human beings from God, themselves, each other and the earth is brought into sharp and brutal focus by war. In Christ, all things are reconciled, all dimensions of our alienation are addressed. This book helps us better to understand what it means for us in a world at war, if we are truly to find our share with Christ in the ministry of reconciliation.

Canon David W. Porter
Coventry Cathedral, August 2009

INTRODUCTION AND ACKNOWLEDGMENTS

The theme I address in this book is the question of how Christians relate to war and peace. More specifically, I examine whether there are principles to comprehend and examples we can follow when faced with the horrors of war and the elusiveness of peace, and we ask ourselves the question: what can a person do?

This book is based on four lectures I gave in November 2008 in the London Lectures series, started by Dr John Stott over thirty years ago. I am grateful to the London Lectures Trust for their confidence in assigning this task to me, and for their support as I prepared and gave the lectures. It has been a privilege to follow in the footsteps of the distinguished speakers who have trodden this path, fascinating to research the issues in more depth than I had previously done, and educational to respond to challenging questions and contributions at the end of each lecture.

Many others have helped to make this book a reality, and I freely acknowledge my debt to all of them. My past and current colleagues at Concordis International – Edward Christow, Stephen Stordy, Michael Schluter, Mark Simmons, Tim Hayden-Smith, Chris Wake, Ellen Roberts, Adam Backhouse, Lucian Harriman and Janet Seaby – are people from whom I have learned a great deal as we have worked together, as indeed I have from those in the sister organizations, the Jubilee Centre and the Relationships Foundation. The Trustees of Concordis International, under whose governance I have served for six years, and especially the two Chairmen – Viscount Crispin Brentford and Professor Sheila Wirz – have provided support and wisdom through those years of sometimes nail-biting operational and financial uncertainty. They have also given me the freedom, not only to prepare the lectures and this book, but also to pursue research in my 'spare' time at the University of Cambridge for the past three years.

The two freedoms are linked, because my part-time studies for a Master's degree and now for a PhD have enabled me to gain some inkling of what our work at Concordis is about and, I hope, to have something to say about it in the chapters that follow. I am therefore especially grateful to my supervisor at Cambridge, Dr Philip Towle, who still waits patiently for the fruits of my research. More directly involved in the production of the book have been Eleanor Trotter and her colleagues at Inter-Varsity Press, who have helped enormously to keep me on track, and whose real work starts when I breathe a sigh of relief and put my feet up. In the process, Ralph Ireland and Martyn Eden voluntarily gave up valuable time to make helpful comments on the manuscript. Most of all, I would like to thank my son Matthew, my daughter Gabriela, and especially my wife Ingrid, who have all supported and encouraged me more than they can ever know.

I have tried in the notes to each chapter (listed at the back of this book) to show where the ideas have come from, both in order to help those who wish to delve deeper and to be fair to the original thinkers. However, we all learn from many and varied sources, and sometimes we forget. So from others who see their ideas in the following pages, I beg forgiveness.

This is a subject matter in which much is at stake. I listened recently to a radio dramatization of a classic Nevil Shute novel of 1957: *On the Beach*. A nuclear war has wiped out all animal life in the northern hemisphere, as a result of nuclear proliferation in smaller nations. Progressively, the nuclear fallout spreads southward, eventually leaving only those in southern Australia alive. And then even they die. It is a reminder, and one that is easily forgotten by those of us who have lived through decades of peace, of the importance of the subject. We all know this, but where we may differ is on how we should deal with these issues.

On the Beach is also a reminder to me of aspects of warfare that I am not covering in depth in this book. I will be leaving out whole swathes of territory that some might think I should try to capture. I think it best to work towards answering one basic question: what does it mean to be a peacemaker? So I deliberately concentrate on how Christians can involve themselves in working towards peace and stability, focusing quite tightly on the role of outsiders in twenty-first-century violent conflict. Some may therefore reach the end of the book with a feeling that it has not covered as much of the broader subject as they would have wanted, that there are depths they wished I had plumbed. However, the book is founded on the experience and learning that I have gained. I would not have the temerity to step outside that zone.

This is not an academic book. One of my favourite Peanuts cartoons shows Charlie Brown and his friends lying on their backs watching clouds drift across a sunny sky. When Lucy asks what shapes they can see in the clouds, Linus sees a map of British Honduras, then the profile of a famous painter, then the stoning of Stephen, with the apostle Paul looking on. Charlie Brown has his turn. 'I was going to say I saw a duckie and a horsie,' he says, 'but I changed my mind.' Like Charlie

Brown, I tend towards the practical and down-to-earth rather than the academic heights. Readers who are experts in conflict resolution or international relations will find the level of theory that I will bring into the discussion quite basic, since one of my aims is to help non-specialist Christians better understand how they can apply their faith to these complex matters.

There is a further caveat. This is not intended to be a biblical analysis, but rather an attempt to help Christians make some sense of modern conflict. I wish to avoid the rather pompous suggestion that only Christians have the answers in this field, but instead consciously to take into account the best wisdom available from other traditions. Nevertheless, I am sure that we can shed some of the light of our faith on the complexities of violent conflict. As the book progresses, I will suggest that there is no single or simple answer to these problems. Indeed, I cannot guarantee that any answers I may come up with will be significantly different from those given to us by secular commentators. However, I think it right to try to bring Christian values to bear on these questions. I hope I will show that there are genuine options for Christians to choose, and that although we may feel powerless, God is not.

Peter Dixon
Cambridge
June 2009

1 WAR IN THE TWENTY-FIRST CENTURY

'You will hear of wars and rumours of wars, but see to it that you are not alarmed. Such things must happen, but the end is still to come.'
Matthew 24:6

'For to us a child is born, to us a son is given, and the government will be on his shoulders. And he will be called Wonderful Counsellor, Mighty God, Everlasting Father, Prince of Peace.' Isaiah 9:6

'He makes wars cease to the ends of the earth; he breaks the bow and shatters the spear, he burns the shields with fire.' Psalm 46:9

Walking in Kabul

It was in January 2004, as I picked my way with my new colleague through the half-frozen mud that served as pavement beside a Kabul street, stepping aside to watch a German armoured personnel carrier drive by, that I realized how much my situation was changing. In some ways, I felt safer than if I had been inside the armoured vehicle with the NATO troops. It is true that, despite being wrapped up against the biting cold, we were clearly recognizable as Westerners to anything more than a casual glance. However, we were fairly unobtrusive and did not feel as much like obvious targets as the white four-wheel drive vehicles of the United Nations and relief organizations. Walking was perhaps safer, and often quicker, than sitting in a taxi in the

crawling or stationary Kabul traffic, and we were not following any set patterns. We could have hired a car and driver, but
such luxuries were well above our budget ceiling.

Later, I felt somewhat less safe as an ancient and gnarled
taxi driver took us in his ancient and battered taxi to our
appointment at the heavily fortified United States Embassy. I
am not sure if he could read at all, but if so he certainly could
not read the signs in English on the approaches, warning
of the authority to use deadly force against any perceived
threat. Nor could he read the sign next to the narrow gap
between giant concrete blocks, explaining that it was absolutely and completely forbidden to stop any vehicle in front
of the entrance. So we stopped, dead centre in front of the
gap, because our knowledge of Pashto (an Indo-European
language spoken primarily in Afghanistan and north-western
Pakistan, also known as Afghani) was not quite up to the
challenge of explaining to the driver the urgency of our –
and his – situation. The less-than-gentle exhortations of the
large number of US Marine Corps guards who appeared from
nowhere to instruct us and the driver to 'Get the *** out of
here' were no better understood. There probably could not
have been a more unlikely looking car bomb, but this was not
the time to put forward that particular argument. We disem-
barked from the taxi with alacrity and sent the driver on his
way with a few grubby notes and much gesticulating. I was
not yet well enough acquainted with my colleague to know
how to take his question: 'Should we insist on a receipt?'

There were several lessons for me to learn from this early
experience in my new line of work. After over thirty years as
a Royal Air Force officer, I was in what the military would call
an operational area, but without the protection or support
networks that military personnel would expect as a matter
of course. I was going to have to get used to making risk

assessments in a new way for myself and for those for whom I held responsibility. For emergencies, I would have to depend on common sense, training and travel insurance. Of course, the risks and dangers were different too – much less severe than those faced by any soldier – in my new role with the conflict-resolution and peace-building organization that we eventually named Concordis International.

The other big change for me had to do with resources. Money had been by no means unlimited in my various military positions: the pressure to reduce costs had been constant. However, the very direct linkage between how much we could raise, how much we spent, and what we were able to achieve, was quite new for me as a personal responsibility. This was why we walked and took taxis rather than hiring a vehicle and driver, and why we were staying in a very modest and very cold guest house, heated by temperamental wood-burning stoves that took me back to the Nissen huts of my cadet days. Ironically, when I first started to 'enjoy' these new experiences, I was still formally a serving officer, making use of the generous allocation of 'resettlement' time provided to ease the transition into civilian life. I was still being paid by the RAF for three months while working in my new role – perhaps the reason the Board gave me the job in the first place!

Resource limitations had a much more serious impact than on just our personal comfort and my attractiveness as a prospective employee. Our very limited funds gave us little room for manoeuvre. This fact-finding visit to Afghanistan led to requests from senior Afghans to assist them in developing national consensus between ethnic groups, requests that we had no hope of fulfilling without help from a donor. However, the kind of long-term peace-building work we were being asked to do matched neither the understanding nor the short-term political goals of the international community as

represented by the diplomats and other officials of the United
Nations and the mostly Western countries in Kabul. This was
perhaps unsurprising in view of the short tours of duty these
people undertook in Afghanistan. So the funding applications
we painstakingly prepared met with a negative response, or
no response at all, and our Afghanistan project did not get off
the ground. Today, several years later, the security situation
in the country has deteriorated. British troops are fighting
and dying in Helmand Province, 500 kilometres south-west
of Kabul, and the streets of the capital are much less safe. We
would not now be in a position to operate there in the same
way as in those early days. Who can say whether the work
we were asked to take on would have had a real impact if we
had been able to do it? However, it was an early lesson to me
in the imbalance between the resources available for conflict
resolution and those provided for military purposes.

In those few days in Kabul, at a time of personal transition when I was trying to process a whole range of new
experiences and concepts, I came across many of the issues
in microcosm that this book will try to deal with at greater
length:

- different ways of dealing personally with armed conflict
  and its aftermath
- disparities in power and resources
- varying time horizons
- international norms of humanitarian intervention
- concepts of reconciliation
- the frustration of being unable to pursue a course of
  action that seems self-evidently right.

Although Concordis is not constitutionally a Christian organization, I approached these questions from a Christian view-

point and propose in the following pages, on a much broader canvas, to attempt a Christian 'take' on how an individual can and should engage with armed conflict in the twenty-first century.

I am not the first to examine these matters, particularly in the debate over pacifism, which chapter 2 covers. Others with much greater academic and specialist qualifications, and often with strong convictions in one direction or another, have already done so. The short time in Kabul symbolized a transition for me from a military career to a period of peace-building activity, although not a shift of personal perspective. Moreover, I have in the past few years made it my business to study the fields of international relations and conflict resolution in some depth. I hope, therefore, to give a balanced view, informed by military experience and by rubbing shoulders with international relations academics and the peace-building community, by biblical insights and by secular understanding of war and peace.

Wars and rumours of wars

In the quotations at the head of this chapter, there lies before us the conundrum for the Christian of how to engage with violence and conflict in the world. Jesus tells us to expect wars and rumours of wars in this present age. And we see them. But Jesus is the Prince of Peace, who brings peace and prosperity to the world.

This is in essence another facet of the difficulty of why God allows evil and suffering in the world. It is a question that has been a stumbling block for many who have considered the Christian faith and turned away, shaking their heads. To get to the bottom of it, one needs to take a broader look rather than just consider warfare and violence. I have always found C. S. Lewis to be the author who can put his finger honestly

on the crux of an issue without reducing the answer to platitudes, and one of the most thoughtful but accessible books
on the question is his *The Problem of Pain*.[1] For the purposes
of this book, it will have to suffice to accept that the apparent
inconsistency of the three verses that start this chapter is a
'now-but-not-yet' issue. We have to live in sure and certain
hope of the better future, but that does not imply passivity
in the present; we are not to live in idleness or inactivity.
Strange as it may be when we look at our imperfect and
unimpressive selves, it seems that the way God has decided
to work in the world is not by making wrongdoing – in this
case aggression and violence – impossible for humankind,
but to allow us the opportunity to play our part in making
the world a better place. A great mystery!

The reports of apparently intractable conflicts and
unspeakable atrocities are an aspect of modern and postmodern life that often leaves us confused about who is in
the right, and uncertain in any case about what we can do
about it. At the same time, we have to take seriously the
charge that religion is part of the problem and not part of
the solution.

There are a couple of questions we should ask ourselves
first, to set a framework for what follows: a why and a how.

Firstly, *why* should we work to bring peace and stability? Why not leave combatants with whom we have little
in common to fight it out, especially when the issues being
fought over do not directly affect us, when we do not know
if we can have a positive impact, and when there may be considerable cost involved? I would suggest that the humanity we
have in common under God is the answer. The humanitarian
imperative, although by no means a Christian monopoly, is
a key part of our faith's concern for the poor and helpless.
However, this does not necessarily equate to providing just

humanitarian assistance or aid, which can easily become a prize to be fought over in a conflict. We are called to be peacemakers. So if we can prevent or stop violent conflict, or work towards sustaining an inevitably fragile peace after a ceasefire, is it not our duty to do so?

Secondly, *how* can or should we get involved? There are two main answers to this. We may be in the privileged position of being able to get involved directly. Christians are active in many ways: through peace campaigning, the armed forces, political engagement, the military chaplaincy, diplomacy or reconciliation work, to cite just some examples. Or our involvement can be much more indirect, as we bring Christian values to professional life (as a civil servant, a politician, a business person, an aid worker, a charity donor, etc.), or to our political engagement as a voter or an activist. And most importantly, even if we cannot directly engage, we can play a crucial role through our prayer.

Understanding today's conflicts

Looking at our televisions or newspapers, and seeing what is going on in distant Africa or Asia, we could easily be forgiven for coming to such horrors with a feeling of helplessness. It seems, though, that the place to start is by correctly understanding the issues at stake. If we engage without full understanding in a question like Darfur, Rwanda, Aceh or the so-called Democratic Republic of Congo – whether directly, or indirectly through our support of particular actions – then there is a fair chance that our actions could be misdirected. If nothing else, we should do no harm.

Perhaps the best place to start in trying to understand today's conflicts is to set the scene by establishing some ideas about the international situation in the twenty-first century. Although it would be foolish not to recognize that some things have stayed the same, it is helpful to try to isolate some fundamental changes.

The first major change has been a shift from war *between* states to war *within* states. This is not a clear distinction. It is often difficult to distinguish between interstate and internal conflicts. Indeed, in Africa, many state boundaries are an artificial imposition of the colonial period. Oliver Ramsbotham of the University of Bradford and his colleagues point out that 'most major armed conflicts today are hybrid struggles that spill across the international, state and societal levels'.[2] And definitions can themselves be controversial. When one walks the narrow streets of Jerusalem, it is painfully clear that to call the Israeli–Palestinian conflict either an interstate or a domestic conflict is to make a political assertion.

Despite these ambiguities, most armed conflict since the end of the Cold War has been within rather than between states. Interstate war is not inconceivable; tensions between some states – between India and Pakistan, for example – remain acute, and the potential consequences of war between well-armed states may be high. Nevertheless, a high incidence of violent conflict within states is a feature of the post-Cold War world.

Secondly, the phenomenon we call globalization has affected the impact of conflict around the world. Internal conflict might, of course, have remained an internal matter, insulated from outside involvement by the protective borders of sovereign states. But this is becoming less and less so. Global politics and international security have been affected since the 1990s by increasing social interaction and economic interdependence. The costs of telephone calls to anywhere in the world have dropped very low in many cases. Indeed, when our daughter in Australia shows off her pet cat to my wife and me, via her Skype-connected webcam, the cost is exactly zero.

Travel is more rapid and affordable, and we can see in real time what is happening on the other side of the world, or at least a version of it that somebody else wishes us to see. In parallel, as Ian Clark suggests, globalization has been accompanied by fragmentation, as the increased influence and wider networks of social groups below the state level have eroded the power of the state.[3] The Facebook phenomenon is one very visible sign of this type of network.

Thirdly, the growing emphasis on human rights and human security, based on a way of thinking called cosmopolitanism, has made it less feasible for a state to seal its borders against international pressures. This has culminated in the adoption by the United Nations of the 'Responsibility to Protect' principle, of which more later.

So the state system that has existed since the Peace of Westphalia of 1648 (the two peace treaties of Osnabrück and Münster, resulting from the first modern diplomatic congress and initiating a new order in central Europe based on the concept of state sovereignty) has been eroded in the twentieth and twenty-first centuries, as complex forms of warfare have developed that are not simply one or more states fighting one or more other states for the control of territory.

The features of these 'new wars' have been helpfully described by Mary Kaldor of the London School of Economics.[4]

- Firstly, they have increasingly involved a range of so-called non-state actors as well as state authorities, both above and below state level, among them the hundreds of armed groups and militias that we see on our television screens.
- Secondly, the issues at stake have not just been territorial, but have involved ideology, resources and identity.

- Thirdly, the primary victims of these conflicts are often the civilians, and this is not simply a side-issue, brought about by their relative weakness. Civilians are often deliberately targeted to mobilize group identity and to emphasize the 'otherness' of a different group. And this is why genocide, rape, ethnic cleansing and displacement, and other human rights abuses are not just tragic side-effects of war. They are conscious techniques of warfare based on the dehumanization of a group that is ethnically or socially defined. As we will see later, the Christian faith must have something to say about this.
- Finally, this type of conflict can be seen as the underside of globalization, linked in complex and confusing ways to state weakness, international criminality, smuggling, drug production, war economies, so-called 'informal taxation' and international terrorism. And that is where it affects us most directly.

Such social changes can of course affect the livelihoods and even survival of civilian populations in their already impoverished and precarious existence. People are displaced from their homes, often to urban areas, which can also lead to political radicalization as new social groupings develop and traditional leadership structures are eroded. But the instability in far-off territories can also affect our own prosperity in our comfortable Western societies. All of these changes must impact the way Christians think about violent conflict.

Much work has gone into studying these intra-state conflicts, and we will just skim the surface here. Edward Azar, for example, wrote in the 1970s about 'protracted social conflict', thinking particularly of the Arab–Israeli conflict and the civil war in his homeland of Lebanon.[5] This type of conflict is not over quickly. The level of animosity remains high, but fluctuates over a long period. The conflict tends to spill over and cover a broad spectrum of interrelated issues and, worst of all, there are powerful forces of equilibrium resisting shifts both towards war and towards peace. Over decades, the strained relations fluctuate between periods of outright war and times when peaceful resolution seems tantalizingly close, but the tense status quo keeps being re-established.

Such a conflict is self-fuelling. Animosities are aroused by hostile acts that reinforce group identity and the negative perception of the 'other'. This type of conflict is also often called 'intractable', not meaning that it is totally permanent, but that it affects fundamental identities and needs, and therefore can not be resolved by normal compromise and mediation of interests. What are needed are changed attitudes and modified institutions in the society. These deep-rooted conflicts can not be resolved simply by negotiations, but require much deeper remedies like structural change to root out societal inequities.[6] This is where the connection between peace and justice starts to enter the frame.

What is causing it?

There are many different ways of thinking about the causes of internal conflict, rooted in different bodies of thought, including nationalism, Marxism, realism and social-psychological analysis, and each emphasizing different aspects. Ultimately, the Christian should not be surprised that such conflict takes place in a fallen world of injustice and sin. And of course the Bible has one or two things to say about the causes of conflict. 'What causes fights and quarrels among you? Don't they come from your desires that battle within you? You want something but don't get it. You kill and covet, but you cannot have what you want.'[7] However, it is not enough to depend on verses like these. We need to recognize

a broader range of mutually reinforcing causes, interconnected in complex ways.

Ethnic, cultural and religious identity are perhaps the most
commonly cited causes of conflict, and we often leave it at
that. Yet groups defined in this way can develop grievances or
reinforce their identity because of unequal economic development or access to livelihoods and resources, often caused
by marginalization of a region of a country, and power differentials between ethnic groups. Where high-value resources
like oil, precious metals or minerals are available, competition for control of them can drive violent conflict, often called
'the curse of riches'. Environmental pressures on livelihoods
have their greatest effect on the poor, and increase income
differentials. Inequities are in many cases part of a colonial
legacy, where elites have been strengthened or created from
one ethnic group to improve the governability of colonies:
a particularly British skill. Also, the construction of states
by colonial rulers, with artificial borders that do not match
existing ethnicity, has often led to shared cross-border ethnic
identity and, connected to this, regional rivalries between
neighbouring states.

International pressures have also played their part.
Ideological differences nurtured during the Cold War may
not be so much in the news today, but they continue to play
a role. More obvious still in the current international political
climate are the perceptions of inequality between different
parts of the world and the angry resistance to US or Western
global dominance. International terrorism is fuelled by this,
while the global counter-terrorism response is at the very
least a distraction from any international measures that might
calm intra-national conflict. The international linkages made
possible by low-cost efficient communications also encourage international crime and 'conflict entrepreneurship', and

make it easier to turn a profit through shadow economies. One very damaging aspect of this is the widespread availability and low cost of weapons.

If the relationships between these causes of conflict seem chaotic and confusing, it is no accident. That is how things are.

Religious identity and warfare

Returning to the question of religion and war, I hope that the discussion of the causes of violent conflict above has gone some way towards answering the question of whether religion is part of the problem. If you are interested in considering this further, you might want to read *The Gods of War* by Meic Pearse.[8] Pearse suggests that ancient empires established some level of stability by taking religion seriously, whereas the modern secular democratic model, which thinks it has progressed beyond religion, has destabilized the situation. These ideas deserve more space than this book can devote to them, and are supported by Vinoth Ramachandra in the chapter on 'Myths of Religious Violence' in his book *Subverting Global Myths.*[9] He points out that secularists have used the attacks perpetrated by Islamists on 11 September 2001 to suggest that religion inevitably leads to violence, ignoring wars of the twentieth century caused by atheistic regimes and, in more recent times, church opposition to the 2003 invasion of Iraq.

Nevertheless, we must acknowledge historical wrongs. The histories of Christianity and Islam are littered with examples of massacres and abuses. We should also recognize the differences of perception that lead us to misunderstand others' religious, political and social identity. We need to understand, for example, that the Western separation of religion from ethnicity and politics is simply a foreign concept to many Muslims. Equating 'Western' with 'Christian' is common, even if we may sometimes suspect that it is a convenient misconception. It is therefore very easy for religion to be manipulated for political purposes, reinforcing the negative connotations of identity differences and the real or perceived inequities described above as causes of conflict.

Ultimately, it is up to us to ensure that religion – or rather, our Christian faith – is part of the solution and not a cause of violent conflict. We are called to work for peace. However, the biblical understanding of peace – captured in Hebrew as *šālôm* and in Greek as *eirēnē* – is broader, deeper and richer than the English word is able to describe. We shall see this in later chapters. To work towards this kind of peace will require a good understanding of issues, a willingness not to stereotype other groups and a degree of humility in seeking to understand other perspectives. We can approach these problems with a realistic but hopeful Christian attitude. We know that we live in a fallen world and that we can always expect difficulty. But we are still called to work in the world for good, and we know that the ultimate sovereignty is God's sovereignty.

> We are called to work for peace. However, the biblical understanding of peace – captured in Hebrew as *šālôm* and in Greek as *eirēnē* – is broader, deeper and richer than the English word is able to describe.

To summarize one of the foundations of this book, there is a form of warfare that is not totally new but has more or less prevailed since the end of the Cold War. It often involves a battle for power and for control of resources within a state, potentially spilling over into and embroiling neighbouring states. Religious identities and ideological issues may play a major role and may be exploited in the competition for the support of the people, but real or perceived unequal access to resources is likely to be a significant driver of conflict. Increasingly, as the distinction between combatants and non-combatants has been eroded, the impact of conflict on civilians has increased. These pressures fall disproportionately on the poor and on vulnerable groups such as women and children, who have limited coping options. Improved global communication has made this suffering more obvious to populations in our more privileged societies, and increased the pressure on governments to prevent it.

Resolving these deep-rooted conflicts needs much deeper changes in society than just putting an end to the fighting, as we shall see later when we consider some of the more subtle and nuanced forms of action. The most immediate reaction of many onlookers, though, is to demand some kind of military intervention, so in the next three chapters we will look at armed force and Christian attitudes to it.

2 THE CHRISTIAN AND WAR

'When elephants fight, it's the grass that gets trampled.' Kikuyu saying

When I was a young boy, my grandfather used to tell me the story of how he was incapacitated by chlorine gas, probably at the Second Battle of Ypres in 1915. Supposedly, he awoke in the mortuary. ''Ere, Bert, this one's alive,' the attendant said, according to Grandad, when he used to recount the unverifiable anecdote with some delight. I never checked on it, but had things gone differently, I suppose I would not be here to tell the tale.

In one of the best-known poems of the First World War, *Dulce et Decorum Est*, Wilfred Owen brings home the horrors of war. The Latin phrase of the title, drawn from a poem by Horace, asserts that 'it is sweet and right to die for your country'. But if, says Owen to the reader, graphically describing the impact of chlorine gas on the men at the front, if you could see and hear the reality:

> My friend, you would not tell with such high zest
> To children ardent for some desperate glory,
> The old Lie; Dulce et Decorum est
> Pro patria mori.[1]

This is a powerful corrective to the glorification of war that was a feature of the pre-war period and the early part of

the war, continuing the jingoism that became prevalent in
the nineteenth century partly under the influence of social
Darwinism. I hope there are few Christians today who glam-
orize war in that way.

Yet there is a sense in which it *is* honourable to put your
life on the line for friends, family or even country. Jesus said,
'Greater love has no-one than this, that he lay down his life
for his friends',[2] and in a different context he is the supreme
example.

War is nasty, brutal and distressing, and we are right to
emphasize its horrors. But it is also right to acknowledge the
variety of attitudes to warfare that Christian believers have
held over the centuries, and to recognize that this debate
continues today. The aim of this chapter is to look at how
different Christian views on the employment of armed force
hold up in the face of the complications presented by the
twenty-first century. This means looking at two intertwined
questions. The first is the matter of an individual Christian's
personal involvement, and the second is the much broader
ethical question of starting, fighting and ending wars. I will
look at the attempts to bring up to date the framework that
has traditionally regulated the debate for many Christians:
the Just War tradition. How, for example, does Just War
stand up against the existence of weapons of mass destruction
and the prevalence of international terrorism?

There are clearly major tensions between the views of
Christian pacifists, who hold that it is always wrong to use
violence, and those of other Christians, who claim that there
are circumstances in which it is not only right to fight, but
also an essential form of service. Between the two stretches a
spectrum of opinions, including those who genuinely see the
merits of both points of view, those who see nuclear, bio-
logical and chemical weapons as a particular exception, and

even those who are undecided on the issue, perhaps because they have never been forced by personal involvement in warfare or military matters to give the subject much thought.

I do not plan to rehearse again in detail the arguments for and against a pacifist viewpoint. This chapter will be neither a biblical analysis nor an exhaustive academic treatment. Others on both sides of the argument have done these things very effectively. To nail my own colours to the mast, I am not and never have been a pacifist. Nor has my military career, though long and satisfying, been particularly distinguished. So there are others much more qualified than I to give a spirited defence of pacifism or a detailed explanation of the problems facing a Christian soldier.[3] However, I have in a sense seen both sides of the coin that we are to render to Caesar. So I hope that a balanced and informed explanation of the issues may help to shed some light for those with a less specialized knowledge on a difficult area of our shared faith.

In trying to shed this light, I owe a debt to the many writers on the Just War tradition, especially the editors and authors of *The Price of Peace*, which I recommend to those who wish to dig deeper.[4] The book owes much to the legacy of Major-General the Reverend Ian Durie, who was one of the driving forces behind the conference five years ago that led to the *Price of Peace* volume. Ian did not attend the conference that he helped to plan. Working in Romania helping to restore a Christian ethic to the post-Communist armed forces, he was tragically killed in a traffic accident. I worked on the same project a couple of years earlier, and I shudder when I remember taking the same hair-raising minibus journey, possibly with the same youthful driver.

The Price of Peace has been critically appraised by Tony Kempster of the Anglican Pacifist Fellowship, who notes the lack of consensus among the authors about contemporary issues like the Iraq War, and criticizes the unclear nature of Just War because 'many Christians will look to the Churches for guidance when next the war drums begin to beat'.[5] Kempster suggests a dynamic reworking of the Just War tradition that will lead back to full-fledged pacifism.

As is the case for most people, my own perspectives on these questions have developed from many inputs, not least my personal life experience.

Pacifism and the Just War tradition

When, as an eighteen-year-old student at the University of Bristol, I made a firm and life-changing Christian commitment, I was already signed up to a career as a Royal Air Force pilot. So I was faced in an immediate, personal and practical way with the questions of war and violence that theologians have studied for centuries. At that point, if I had decided that it was wrong for a Christian to serve in the military, I could have chosen without too much complication to walk away from my planned career and taken a different track. I did not do so, and I was helped in my immature but serious consideration of these questions by the wisdom of others who had gone through the same process. The work of the organization now known as the Armed Forces Christian Union, of which I eventually served a term as Chairman, was particularly helpful in this. I have also been extremely fortunate, over thirty years, that my decision has not been seriously tested by the messy, horrific and ambiguous business that war inevitably is. So I listen to Christians who refuse to bear arms with respect and admiration. But I cannot agree with them.

However, the other side of the coin for me has been the work that I took on six years ago when I left the Royal Air Force. Chapter 7 describes the work of Concordis International, where I have spent the past six years in conflict prevention, conflict resolution and peace-building, focusing mainly on Sudan, including Darfur. I have therefore talked with many, Christians and others, who wish to put their visceral abhorrence of violence and war into some form of practical application. So I have become intimately familiar with both sides of the debate. I also have to admit to being a natural fence-sitter, with an innate ability not to take sides in any argument, but rather to understand both viewpoints. While this is probably something of an advantage in the work Concordis does, it can be infuriating to protagonists who know for sure that all of the evidence is on their side.

Christian pacifists cite Jesus' injunction to Peter in the garden of Gethsemane to put up his sword, and a number of his other sayings, to suggest that Christians should not use violence. The martyrdom of Stephen at the hands of a stone-throwing mob, and the statements of Paul, such as that in the first letter to the Corinthians, give believers an example to follow in the face of violence against the person.[6] Twentieth-century Christian pacifists, prominent among them Dr Martin Luther King, have been dissatisfied with the passivity implied by the biblical and some early Christian examples; they have developed the concept of non-violent resistance. Indeed, their claims that such action is often more effective than violence, particularly in the case of resistance to a repressive regime, enjoy strong support. However, as we will consider below, subjugation of a people and violence against the individual are not the only situations we may have to deal with. So we have to look at the more general question.

The debate over whether it is right for a Christian to take up arms has rumbled on for centuries. In the days when Jesus walked in Palestine, the issue was an immediate and poignant one. The Jewish and Palestinian victims of an often brutal Roman occupation were faced with the question of whether

they should resist and, if so, by what means. In this context of
a generally resentful and rebellious Jewish society, the New
Testament does not permit the use of violence in resisting
the Romans or their puppet rulers, or in fighting the injustices of occupation. So when, in the context of taxation, Jesus
was asked his view on giving tribute to the Roman emperor,
his typically complex, somewhat ambiguous and no doubt
irritating answer emphasized the distinction between God's
kingdom and Caesar's, but did not forbid cooperation with
the Roman occupiers.[7] Indeed, his attitude to the occupying
Roman officers and soldiers was generally positive when he
encountered them.[8]

Despite Jesus' sympathy with officers and soldiers, many
claim that the early Christians' attitude to military service
was overwhelmingly negative. However, we must see this
against the background of the position of Christians in
Roman imperial society. From the first days of the church,
but particularly under Nero following the Great Fire of Rome
and during the reign of Diocletian, Christians faced persecu-
tion throughout the Empire. Their refusal to make public
sacrifices to Roman gods, including the emperor as a god, led
to thousands of martyrdoms. It is hard to imagine how they
could serve such a state in its army, where allegiance to the
pagan gods was expected. Nevertheless, there is evidence of
at least a small number of Christian soldiers in some legions,
although it is not clear whether these included only those
who had been converted while serving.[9] Perhaps they were
following Paul's advice to the Corinthians, to remain in the
situation they were in when they were called.[10] That many
of them were persecuted is clear, but what is not so obvious
is that the oft-cited examples of Christian pacifists were persecuted for their refusal to fight rather than for their faith in
general and rejection of pagan worship in particular.

Overall, we should not necessarily assume that pre-Constantinian Christians were united either in refusal to bear arms or in opposition to Roman rule. As in the New Testament, the situation appears to have been much more nuanced. More or less at the same time as evidence appears of increasing numbers of Christian soldiers, a debate develops and the Christian pacifism apparently espoused by writers like Tertullian, Origen and Hippolytus becomes more prevalent. Yet this debate was never a major controversy, and the objection to military service remained as much to do with enforced idolatry as with killing.

The situation of Christians changed dramatically when the Emperor Constantine legalized Christian worship throughout the Empire, through the Edict of Milan of AD 313. Now Christians were in the ascendancy. They became part of the Roman establishment and, although Constantine was not in a position to ban paganism, Christians were soon serving at the highest levels of government. Thus identification of the state with Christianity, and the blending of the two in a form of civic religion, was at its height under Constantine. This is something we see continued in the Islamic concept of the *umma* (the whole community of Muslims), but also almost subconsciously in the modern USA.[11]

Back in the Constantine period, theologians were grappling in different ways with the questions posed by believers' allegiances both to God and to the supposedly Christian empire. One striking example is a letter from Ambrose of Milan to the Emperor Theodosius, whose troops had slaughtered 7,000 Thessalonians following a riot in which the Roman commander had been killed. Ambrose ordered the Emperor to humble himself before God and do penance for this sin. And the Emperor did so.[12]

Just a little later than Ambrose, Just War thinking was

further developed by the Christian thinker with whom we most often associate it. Augustine of Hippo aimed both to reassure Christians that there were circumstances in which it was legitimate to fight in the armies of the secular Roman civil state, and to set limits to their behaviour if they did so. This is already very like the classic distinction between *jus ad bellum* – the justice of going to war – and *jus in bello* – regulating the means that may be used in fighting a Just War.

Latin terms in the Just War tradition	
jus ad bellum	'rules' about going to war
jus in bello	'rules' about behaviour during war
jus post bellum	'rules' about the situation after war

Augustine emphasized the need to wage war only for just purposes and not for gain or as an exercise of power, the need for a proper authority to authorize war, and the need for love as a motivation. He saw lust for power as the real evil, rather than war itself. This rather convoluted quote shows his complex thinking:

> Peace should be the object of your desire. War should be waged only as a necessity and waged only that through it God may deliver men from that necessity and preserve them in peace. For peace is not to be sought in order to kindle war, but war is to be waged in order to obtain peace. Therefore even in the course of war you should cherish the spirit of a peacemaker.[13]

Augustine asserted that the authority of the state derives from the superior authority of 'the One True God' and may – indeed should – for that reason be obeyed. Some 700 years after Augustine's death, Thomas Aquinas further developed this concept of legitimate authority, at a time when a powerful church sought to regulate the affairs of a range of secular rulers.

Progressively, though, the balance of power between the church and the 'princes' (the legitimate rulers of states) shifted. As state power increased and that of the church decreased, Francisco de Vitoria and Hugo Grotius developed the theory further, with two main results: an increasing attempt to codify Just War concepts in positive law, and a shift away from Christian theological underpinnings towards an appeal to the morality of natural law. Eventually, writers like Christian Wolff and Emerich de Vattel, in the context of the development of the nation-state, tried to exclude the morality of war from any international positive law. These developments cannot be disentangled from the philosophical influence of the Enlightenment.

Thus Just War theory became increasingly seen as irrelevant to the positive law related to armed conflict, which developed – for example, through the Kellogg-Briand Pact of 1928 and Article 51 of the UN Charter – more in the direction of the 'illegality' of any war other than in self-defence, and was based on the defence of sovereignty in and of itself without needing to justify its legitimacy. Nevertheless, the conventions of war-fighting in legal codes like the Geneva Conventions are based on Just War theory's *jus in bello* provisions.

More recently, Michael Walzer has tried to provide a secular philosophical underpinning to Just War tradition on the foundation of communitarian thinking.[14] He develops helpful aids to thinking about moral choices in warfare, including the definitions of combatants and legitimate targets. Much of this thought does not differ significantly from traditional Christian Just War tradition, although the way Walzer updated it to modern problems like terrorism, guerrilla war and nuclear weapons is useful, so that, ironically, some modern churchmen have made use of Walzer's 'secular' arguments.

Just War tradition today

We have already observed that there are two broad categories of moral reasoning in the Just War tradition: going to war and actual fighting.[15]

In deciding when a war may be started, we need to recognize that war will cause great suffering. Many therefore say that going to war should be a last resort, after all other means of resolving the dispute have been tried or at least genuinely explored. However, there is a danger that seeking all other alternatives first may just provide excuses not to do the right thing, as most would suggest was the case for Neville Chamberlain in Munich in 1938. So perhaps the conditions should be as follows.

- One test should be whether war is the *only* way to right the wrong.[16]
- War should only be undertaken for a just cause, such as to correct a major evil or to counter aggression.
- The decision-making authority must be legitimate. In Augustine's day, as already mentioned, this meant the legitimate ruler of the state, the 'prince'. What it means today is disputed, and we will go into that in greater detail in the next chapter.
- The use of force is only legitimate if the purpose is to correct the wrong or injustice that has been done – that is, right intention.
- The criterion variously known as 'limited ends', 'relative evil' or 'comparative justice' is disputed, because it

suggests that going to war is an evil, albeit a lesser one. But the tradition has always intended that the suffering or injustice corrected must outweigh that caused by the war itself; it could be called a form of proportionality.

- There must be a reasonable probability of success, before setting out on the dangerous path of warfare, as Jesus suggests in the parable in Luke 14 when he speaks about the king who counts the cost before going to war, even though he draws a different lesson from the story.[17]

This is not a secondary school examination with a 60% pass mark. Under the Just War tradition, all of these criteria should be met before a war is started. But to use the criteria as a simple checklist, as a self-justifying means of salving the conscience or as ammunition in the argument against domestic political opponents, misses the point. Properly used, they provide an opportunity to make a genuine examination of one's own motives and information sources.

Once the decision to go to war has been made, the Just War tradition has a lot to say about the way war is waged. First, the commander or soldier has to discriminate between combatants and non-combatants, and this is enshrined in military law in most modern armies. How we define non-combatants can be disputed, but it would, for example, include disarmed prisoners and civilians who are not involved in the war effort. Although it is accepted that civilians may be hurt in attacking a legitimate military target, they must not be deliberately targeted and every effort must be made to reduce the risk to them. Secondly, the principle of proportionality requires a belligerent to weigh the degree of force used against the injustice that has been done and the potential military or strategic gain. What this means in practice is that the force used must be the minimum required to achieve the military objective. Indeed, some who have written about Just War have included 'minimum force' as a third criterion. Here we will remain with the two mentioned, but they obviously interact with each other. Not using disproportionate force, for example, will help to reduce the chance that non-combatant civilians will suffer.

Even more than the *jus ad bellum* criteria, this is not a simple checklist. It is a set of interdependent considerations to be taken into account by every commander, soldier, sailor or airman when thinking about how to conduct military operations. But do they still apply today? I hope it will be clear from the beginning of this chapter that I believe the answer to be 'yes'. But let me restate my reasons.

First, I would like to suggest that I do not find the case for Christian pacifism persuasive, although I hold honest pacifists in great respect. Pacifists rightly argue that war is a horror and rarely the best way of resolving disputes. And when war has started, history shows us that even if one side can claim to be in the right, the way they prosecute the war can degenerate. Many would argue that this was the case with the deliberate targeting of cities by Allied bombers in 1939–45. 'They did it first' may seem a powerful argument in a schoolboys' fight in the playground, but it cannot prevail in warfare.

However, it seems clear to me that our God is a God of justice as well as a God of peace, and the God of the New Testament is not different from the God of the Old Testament. There

. . . our God is a God of justice as well as a God of peace, and the God of the New Testament is not different from the God of the Old Testament.

will indeed come a time when 'nation will not take up sword against nation' and we will 'beat. . . swords into ploughshares'.[18] But the end days, when God will judge between nations, are not here yet. For now,

he has instituted government to maintain justice, to administer punishment and to defend the poor and needy.[19] As Paul
instructed the Romans,[20] within certain bounds – essentially
that we put obedience to God ahead of obedience to government when the two are in conflict – it is a Christian's duty to
support this, even at great personal cost, whether by serving in
the military or in other ways that we will explore later. We also
learn from Paul: 'Do not take revenge, my friends, but leave
room for God's wrath, for it is written "It is mine to avenge;
I will repay," says the Lord.' [21] Thus, although personal vengeance is to be abhorred, a legitimate government has not just
a right but a duty to administer justice internally, to defend its
citizens and even – for instance, in response to a request from
a weaker nation for help – to fight against injustice outside
its borders. C. S. Lewis points out that the command to non-
resistance applies absolutely to injuries against an individual,
but the situation changes completely when injury to others
enters the picture.[22] Although it is not always possible to
show biblical proof-texts for the Just War tradition, it has been
derived from Scripture to develop biblical principles about
how we wage war: for instance, about right intention, and
excluding retaliation for the purpose of revenge.

In the international system currently in place, where a
world government does not hold authority, the 'right authority' remains the sovereign state, constrained and restrained
by the body of international law, the network of international
treaties and the (albeit imperfect) collection of United Nations
Security Council Resolutions. As permanent members of the
Council can veto resolutions if national interest so demands, it
is perhaps unreasonable always to require a Security Council
resolution as a precondition for military action. Now, this
could be seen as carte blanche for almost any adventure,
and recent history shows that governments need to be very

cautious about bypassing the Security Council. However, this is where the wisdom of our Christian forebears becomes helpful, in the form of the Just War tradition.

This is easy to say, but in practice we will be faced with complex situations, we will find that others hold strongly to views different from ours and we will be genuinely uncertain of the right path to follow. That is one reason why I think God may call some Christian believers to follow in the footsteps of the many thoughtful, courageous and prayerful Christian commanders and soldiers. This brings us full circle to the question of the individual Christian's responsibility to fight or not to fight. Whether or not you agree with my point of view here, we all need to have sympathy for those who are placed in the position of making such decisions of life and death, and to hold them in our prayers even when we think they are wrong.

One area where the difficulties and ambiguities are excruciatingly acute is the question of weapons of mass destruction, where the principles of proportionality and discrimination of non-combatants seem to have been thrown out of the window. Nuclear pacifism, asserting that this particular class of weapons brings in an entirely new moral dimension, itself derives from Just War principles. In a sense, this is not a new problem. As I have mentioned before, the same questions can be applied to the Allied bombing campaigns against Germany during the Second World War. Apart from suggesting that the general principles need to be applied to each situation, I am not sure that I can add much value to this long-running debate other than pointing to helpful sources.[23] Indiscriminate use of weapons against non-combatants is wrong, but we are then, for instance, faced with the problem that nuclear weapons can not be 'uninvented', and that to give them up unilaterally is unlikely to lead to a greater good.

The Just War tradition, then, is not a hard and fast set of rules to be slavishly followed. Rather, it is a useful tool to help us in our thinking about war and violence. Used in this way, it may ironically be well suited to our postmodern age of relativistic morality and situational ethics. Now let's turn it to this purpose in some very topical situations.

3 JUST WAR ON TERROR?

'The battle is now joined on many fronts. We will not waver; we will not tire; we will not falter; and we will not fail.' George W. Bush

'Even peace may be purchased at too high a price.' Benjamin Franklin

'It is an unfortunate fact that we can secure peace only by preparing for war.' John F. Kennedy

Is Just War just about war?

This may seem a foolish question, but it is a fair one. Politicians both deliberately use and deliberately avoid the word 'war' when it suits them, so the definition of war is not quite as clear as we might wish. Can we apply the Just War tradition to today's violent insurgencies, to humanitarian interventions and to the so-called 'Global War on Terror'? We will deal with the first two more fully later, but here we will use the reaction to the infamous attacks in September 2001, on the Twin Towers in New York and on the Pentagon, as an example of how we can use Just War to help our thinking. I do not aim to make political points about the invasion of Afghanistan or Iraq, something others have done at length.

The 'helicopter view' of this chapter contrasts with the very direct form of involvement in warfare considered in chapter 2 when we looked at the interconnected questions of whether and when it may be right for an individual Christian to take up arms, as well as considering what criteria decision-makers should apply when deciding whether to go to war, and how commanders and soldiers should fight that war.

An example: the Global War on Terror

Some think that the use of Just War ideas to argue for or against the 'War on Terror' has brought the tradition into bad repute. However, I will set that aside and use the War on Terror to illustrate the more modern third element of Just War, always implied in the first two – *jus ad bellum* and *jus in bello* – but only recently made more explicit under the name of *jus post bellum* ('rules' about the situation after war).

The events of 9/11 caused a fundamental shift in the US Administration's attitudes, and a new National Security Strategy was prepared.[1] This included prosecuting what was eventually described as the 'long war' against international terrorism. In launching its War on Terror with understandably strong public support, the Bush administration claimed the right to intervene anywhere in the world and use any means to counter international Islamist terrorism. This campaign, although it included a range of measures more associated with policing, was deliberately characterized as a war. We therefore have a right to look at the campaign through the lens of the Just War tradition, especially as President Bush often used religious language. Despite Michael Walzer's attempts to develop a secularized version of Just War, the tradition's ultimate foundation rests with Augustine's attempt to guide Christians regarding their duties to the secular Roman state. If only because of the religious rhetoric used, we should look to Just War tradition as the potential foundation for President Bush's actions.

As we have seen, Just War concepts form the basis of much current international and military law. Yet we should use the tradition as it was intended: not as a legalistic checklist to follow, but rather as a set of principles to guide thinking and discussion about the complex moral issues involved in starting and conducting warfare. On this basis, the Just War tradition is hard pressed to provide a foundation for some aspects of the War on Terror. In particular, the light of the concepts of *jus ad bellum* and *jus in bello* needs to illuminate the invasion of sovereign states and the treatment of prisoners.

Specifically, it seems clear that neither going to war in Iraq in particular (claimed or implied by the US Administration to be a part of the War on Terror) nor undertaking the War on Terror in general offered a reasonable chance of success. Nor is the doctrine of preventive warfare easy to justify, and the distinction between combatants and non-combatants has been seriously blurred.

The comprehensive ideas developed immediately after 9/11 for fighting international terrorism included police action, military activity, intelligence-gathering, border controls and financial measures, all in concert with existing and new allies around the world. We might argue that the softer aspects of reducing terrorist effectiveness, through better understanding and elimination of reasons for opposition to the West, were missing. However, this kind of carefully considered, 'joined-up' counter-terrorist action was, it seemed, exactly what was needed for a sustained campaign to reduce the effectiveness of terrorist networks.

But was it war? And did that matter?

The Bush administration's reasons for using the characterization 'war' may have been to build public support, to legitimize the use of military force under US law or for other reasons. Whatever the motivation, calling it such brought questions of justification into sharper focus, including the justification for using military force for this purpose at all.

The legitimate monopoly of violence claimed by the state, both domestically to maintain order and externally for self-defence, was at the heart of Augustine's concepts. Self-defence appears to have been the argument deployed by President Bush. However, Bush extended the concept of 'defence in depth' to the limit, in that he claimed the right to interdict Al-Qaida wherever it was to be found. In the case of the Afghanistan campaign soon after the 9/11 attacks, this meant an invasion of a sovereign state with the aim of changing its regime. Given the global reach of Al-Qaida from its Afghan bases and the support it was receiving from the Taliban regime, this could perhaps be justified as self-defence.

However, with the right comes the responsibility. This is provided for under Just War tradition by the twin requirements to ensure that the total good outweighs the total evil and to undertake action with a good intention. The latter is perhaps out of fashion in post-Christian, consequentialist versions of Just War theory, but Christians should not lose sight of it. It was certainly a part of Augustine's and Aquinas's conceptions. Modern writers have argued that Augustine's *jus ad bellum* carries with it the requirement for just peace as an outcome of war: in other words, *jus post bellum*. In the case of Afghanistan, Just War made it incumbent on the USA to stabilize the state and assist in its reconstruction, an activity it left to its allies while it continued to try to destroy remnants of the Taliban – with limited success.

This argument is even stronger in the case of the invasion of Iraq. It might be argued that this campaign is nothing to do with the War on Terror, but the Bush administration at least implied that Saddam Hussein and Al-Qaida were connected. Moreover, fighting the Iraq insurgency became part of the War on Terror retrospectively, as jihadists flocked to fight the USA in Iraq. President Bush used this to his advantage, claiming that it was better to fight the terrorists in Iraq than at home. His administration later put more resources and effort into supporting the new Iraqi government, but at the time of the invasion, other aspects of *jus ad bellum* ought to have come into play, in particular the need to set out with a reasonable hope of success. The idealist and triumphalist assumptions underlying the invasion blinded the USA to the possibility of nationalist and religious resistance, and the need to plan for the post-war situation. At the time of writing, it is not clear how the situation in Iraq will develop when President Obama fulfils his pledge to withdraw American combat troops. However, it seems clear that open and honest use of Just War ideas in 2003 would have saved much death and suffering.

We can also apply Augustinian criteria for *jus ad bellum* – going to war – critically to the prosecution of the War on Terror as a whole.

Firstly, although it may be legitimate to act in self-defence, this would normally be in response to a specific act of aggression. Pre-empting such an act when it is imminent, to prevent suffering, is both sensible and responsible. Yet it is far from clear that the preventive action that is now a part of US military doctrine could be justified, with no clear evidence of an imminent attack. It may be that more secret evidence has existed than is publicly available. So what looked like preventive action – trying to prevent an attack that may or may not be going to happen – could actually have been pre-emption, where the threat was real but simply not publicly known. However, exaggeration by the Bush administration of inconclusive intelligence about weapons of mass destruction to justify the invasion of Iraq does not inspire confidence that this is the case.

A second criterion relevant to the broader War on Terror is that there should be a reasonable hope of success. Here,

it is difficult to see how this 'war' could qualify. In his book
With or Against the World?, Jim Skillen rightly argues that it
makes no sense to apply the term 'war' to an open-ended
attempt to control a phenomenon of a 'seemingly ubiqui-
tous and non-specific nature', and that a reasonable hope of
success is impossible when success itself cannot be defined.[2]
The US administration implicitly acknowledged this when it
spoke of the 'long war'.

We can go further. The unintended consequences of the
military aspects of the War on Terror appear to include
increased opposition to the USA in Muslim and developing
world countries. Consequently, the number of 'self-starter
jihadists' has grown; they are unconnected with Al-Qaida but
enthused by information or propaganda, often received via
the Internet. The bombers who attacked a train in Madrid in
March 2004 appear to fall into this category. This counter-
productive effect could perhaps have been foreseen, and goes
against both 'reasonable hope of success' and 'total good
outweighs total harm' aspects of *jus ad bellum*.

The final and most difficult aspect of *jus ad bellum* to be considered is that of rightful authority. The USA could claim to be
perfectly justified in acting in robust self-defence against those
who attack it. In the current global system, there is no superior
authority to give its permission and none is needed. In any
case, the right to self-defence is enshrined in international law.
However, if the means chosen include the invasion of another
sovereign state, then perhaps a greater authority, such as a
UN Security Council Resolution, is needed. This is a point of
tension in the USA, given US scepticism about the effectiveness of the UN and other multinational institutions. Yet it is
counter-productive to ignore the need to work with others in
the military War against Terror when cooperation is needed
in policing and intelligence-sharing, for example.

Relating *jus in bello* criteria – how wars should be fought – to the War on Terror is more straightforward. It seems clear that we need to strike a balance between the obvious need for protection of intelligence sources, maintenance of the element of surprise and effective neutralization of threat, on the one hand, and the rule of law and human rights considerations on the other. This crosses over into questions of policing and jurisdiction, but the Just War tradition does have something to say about these.

In calling the fight against terrorism a war and giving the military a significant combat role in it, the US government took on the difficult responsibility of discriminating between combatant and non-combatant. Those who fight for Al-Qaida do not wear uniform or otherwise distinguish themselves from non-combatants. Nor do they shy away from killing civilians themselves. This makes the job for soldiers and their commanders doubly difficult, but the problem is essentially a familiar one to soldiers of most countries, although perhaps less so to Americans until recently. It is probably unavoidable that military operational training has tended to think in terms of legalistic rules of war rather than a tradition of moral reflection. However, the issues are not essentially different within the Just War context in this 'war' than in other wars. The many grey areas, and outright contraventions in this case, point not just to inadequate training, but to a loss of the principles passed down under the Just War tradition, which should form the bedrock for any regulations and training.

Other arguments to apply the Just War tradition to the War on Terror are more subtle but still powerful. Within Augustine's tradition, the purpose of the armed servants of the state was primarily to restore peace and security to the citizenry. The claimed objective of the War on Terror is exactly this, but the methods used have created a counter-productive effect. We have observed how the fight against terrorism was first developed, immediately after 9/11. This involved a blend of military and non-military measures, in cooperation both between US government agencies and, more importantly, internationally. Such an effort, potentially coordinated through appropriate international institutions, would probably be much more effective in countering international terrorism than a (more or less) unilateral 'war' with doubtful Just War grounding that has seemed to build only resentment.

All of this – deciding about going to war and controlling how it is fought – needs to be seen through the lens of what comes after the fighting. Military planners today often call this the desired end state. For us, though, this is where the idea of *jus post bellum*, the responsibility to create a just peace after the fighting – for friend and foe alike – comes into play. This implies more than empty rhetoric about democracy, and this is where the invasions of Iraq and, to a lesser extent, Afghanistan have fallen down. So, although this *jus post bellum* responsibility was always implied in the Just War tradition, the modern tendency to cite it as a separate factor is helpful.

We all learn. There has been learning, and development of military doctrine, in the US forces in particular as a result of the Iraq war. The US military is very good at learning and applying lessons quickly, and there is now a great deal of recognition that the desired end state in such situations has to include a better peace after the war – that is, the need for *jus post bellum*. There is also recognition that the military instrument is a very blunt one, that it is limited in what it can achieve by itself, and that at best it can only provide the stability for the longer-term work of peace-building to be done, probably by others.

Gaza 2008–9

A situation that can be looked at more briefly is the Israeli bombardment of Gaza, which started in December 2008 and eventually culminated in an invasion by land forces. It shows many parallels with the War on Terror. It too was a reaction to attacks that employed terror tactics. It too involved the use of massively superior power. It too has led to devastation and, arguably, unforeseen consequences.

There is no particular reason why Israelis or Palestinians should make reference to the Just War tradition, even though it is a foundation of modern international law. Both sides consider their cause just, of course, and see that as a sufficient argument. Israel has seen itself as facing an existential threat from outside and from within ever since the birth of the state, while Palestinians see themselves as occupied by a brutal invader, marginalized and oppressed. Often, the Just War tradition is simply used as a stick to beat the enemy, another weapon in a war of words between those who oppose and those who support Israel. This was certainly the case in blogs around the world in early 2009, when supporters of one side or the other attacked the actions of Israel or Hamas (the Palestinian Islamic socio-political organization which since June 2007 has governed the Gaza portion of the Palestinian Territories) in Just War terms and demonstrated the misuse of the tradition. But the breadth and richness of Just War thinking, used in the way already suggested, may help us to work out our own views with a little more clarity.

If we see the situation from a Palestinian perspective, it is possible to imagine how a violent struggle might seem the only way to correct what they see as the injustice wrought by an occupying power. On the other hand, Hamas has often made clear its uncompromising opposition to allowing the presence of Jews anywhere in what it claims as Arab land.

Indeed, it has brought this hostility to bear through rocket attacks over a period of several years, which the Israeli military was determined to stop. Yet the reaction of Israeli forces was widely seen as massively disproportionate. Pictures of Palestinian suffering in Gaza, transmitted across the world, have done immense harm to Israel's external image, even if domestic support for military action in Gaza was strong.

Just as with the War on Terror, the application of Just War's 'reasonable probability of success' criterion turns on how we define success. Short-term military success in ending or reducing Hamas rocket attacks has to be contrasted with the longer-term external political damage. Western Christians are perhaps not a constituency that Israel naturally looks to for support, although it has benefited from such endorsement. That the sympathy of this group seems to be shifting inexorably towards the less powerful Palestinians is perhaps an indication of a wider trend.

With just cause claimed by both sides, and the unquestionable military superiority of Israel making at least a perception of disproportionate violence inevitable, the other Just War criteria are perhaps less significant. However, we should not neglect them if we are to take the tradition seriously. Simply stating that 'the cause is just' does not suffice. Can Christians who side with the Israeli viewpoint, for instance, claim that overwhelming military action in Gaza was the only way of righting the wrongs of Hamas rocket attacks? Or is it possible, for those who see Palestinians as subjugated and repressed, to claim that violence against Israeli civilians was the only course open? Moreover, military action under the Just War tradition should be undertaken with a 'right intention'. Arguably, the intentions of Hamas have been focused as much on destroying Israel, however remote an objective that may be, as on improving the lot of those they were elected to represent. On the other hand, many have claimed that the motives of the Israeli government have been much more complex and far-reaching than simply preventing future rocket attacks.

This is not the place to pass judgement on the relative justice claims of Israelis and Palestinians. As for the War on Terror, the aim here is to identify how one can use Just War as a tool to think through the issues involved.

What's so Christian about Just War?
Using the Global War on Terror and Gaza as topical examples helps us see how the Just War tradition can be applied in practice. Of course, it is easy to do this kind of thing with twenty-twenty hindsight. But apart from recognizing many unintended consequences of militarizing the War on Terror, it seems to place weight on the importance of thinking about what would happen *after* military action.

However, much of what has gone before begs an obvious question, namely, what is Christian about Just War? Certainly, the tradition is not founded on biblical proof texts and it has been appropriated by moral philosophers and international lawyers. However, it does represent a chain of thought by godly men (yes, mostly *men*, but that is the subject of a different book, perhaps by a different author) on how to deal with very difficult issues of life and death.

The church is where Just War thinking should reside, but the secularization and codification of the tradition has obscured this truth. The number of fully convinced pacifists in the church is probably very small. Yet there has developed what Nigel Biggar calls 'practical pacifism' and others call 'functional pacifism'. There seems to be an unexamined assumption that pacifism is the right way; war is so evil that there *must* be some better alternative. Also, some choose to interpret Just War as saying that non-combatants must never be harmed, helped by the claims made for the accuracy of modern weapons. Yet this is in practice an impossibility. Overall, the bar is set so high that, in effect, pacifism is simply assumed and Just War thinking is excluded. This is a real loss, as there has been little success in finding a better alternative.

My purpose in this chapter has been to demonstrate through practical and up-to-date cases that Christians, whether they are soldiers, political decision-makers or simply voters, can use Just War criteria to weigh up the pros and cons for a particular course of action – by themselves or others. None of us will possess full information, or an ability to predict the future events that may cause us to tear up our plans and start again. But we will at least have a moral framework on which to base our thinking, helped by a solid confidence in God's sovereignty as we face the uncertainty of the real world.

None of us will possess full information, or an ability to predict the future events that may cause us to tear up our plans and start again. But we will at least have a moral framework on which to base our thinking, helped by a solid confidence in God's sovereignty as we face the uncertainty of the real world.

There is an unfortunate consequence of public doubt or outright opposition to the British military deployments since 2001 in Iraq and Afghanistan. Many of those risking their lives have not felt that they were supported back home. Possibly one of the most important elements of what is often called the military covenant, this support is crucial. The connection between soldiers and the public they serve is a key part of a properly functioning society. This is one reason why, when we begin to look at involvement in other people's wars, we start in the next chapter with military interventions.

4 INTERVENING IN CONFLICT –
THE MILITARY WAY

'They shall beat their swords into plowshares, and their spears into pruning hooks; nation shall not lift up sword against nation, neither shall they learn war anymore.' Isaiah 2:4, engraved at the entrance of the United Nations headquarters

'Am I my brother's keeper?' Genesis 4:9

Keeping the peace

When we read headlines about the international community's attempts to deal with violent conflicts around the world, we could be forgiven for any pessimism. Yet it is all too easy for the armchair analyst and amateur pundit to pour cold water. Perspectives differ. Pessimism is not present everywhere. Hope exists.

One Sunday in Lent 2009, I watched the boys and girls of All Saints Cathedral Sunday School, Juba, southern Sudan, swaying in unison up the central aisle of the Cathedral in time with their well-rehearsed song, led in the procession and the singing by an eleven-year-old boy. A six-year-old at the rear of the procession seemed a little nonplussed, but overall they were a happy sight. As they reached the altar, lined up and turned to face the congregation, the music – sung in an attractive high-pitched African style – gave way to a joyful ululation and applause from my 500 fellow-worshippers and me. I mused on the future prospects for these children, on religious freedom, and on how similar children might have fared a few years earlier.

On the previous day, I had been working on this chapter under a thatched straw roof in the town of Juba. A gentle cooling breeze blew through the structure, lizards darted across the upright supports and tiny, brightly coloured birds alighted occasionally to catch insects. A peaceful scene. Yet this town and its country have seen more than their share of violence. Civil war has raged in Sudan for all but eleven of the years since independence was gained in 1956. Although violent conflict continues in Darfur, a 'Comprehensive Peace Agreement' brought the north–south war to a tentative end in January 2005, so Juba is peaceful, even if, at seven on a Saturday morning, I could hear a rowdy political rally in the distance.

Taking Sudan as a whole, the mood as I wrote was one of uncertainty and trepidation. This is particularly so in Darfur, where international relief to the displaced has been vastly reduced since the President expelled the dozen or so largest aid agencies, following his indictment by the International Criminal Court for crimes against humanity. The agencies were accused of spying against Sudan, and an atmosphere of mistrust bordering on xenophobia in Khartoum and throughout northern Sudan is making it difficult for the remaining foreign agencies to continue their humanitarian, educational and capacity-building activity.

All of this distracts from the urgent work that needs to be done by the Sudanese, and by those who would wish to support them, to consolidate the 2005 north–south agreement, which could be seen as little more than a six-year ceasefire and an opportunity to put in place the changes that can bring sustained peace. A United Nations force was set up to monitor the agreement, and an African Union force in

Darfur was eventually converted into a 'hybrid' force with a United Nations element. Yet much of the change envisaged by those who drafted the agreement has yet to happen, four years on at the time of writing. Here in the south, the focus is on building a viable southern Sudanese state. There are signs of hope, but there is still a long way to go.

Yet we should not minimize the benefits of having, more or less, brought an end to the fighting. A man who lived in Juba through the civil war years described to me how it had been. The town was a beleaguered outpost of the northern government; large tracts of the south were under rebel control. Southerners living and working in Juba went in fear of being accused of supporting the rebels. Many who were accused were killed or just disappeared. 'People complain about poverty, corruption and the terrible roads in Juba, and ask what happened to the peace dividend,' the man told me, 'but they don't know what they are talking about. At least we can walk around the town without fear.' Another turned to me when I described the packed cathedral. 'That is what freedom brings,' he said. So stopping the fighting may not be everything, but it is something.

Stopping the fighting

The framework used in chapter 2 for thinking about the moral basis of warfare, the Just War tradition often associated with Augustine of Hippo, runs as a thread through the early chapters of this book. In chapter 3 we applied it in quite a theoretical way to current situations. It will appear again here in a supporting role as we try to tease out the factors involved in military intervention in conflict situations in the twenty-first century. The activities variously known as peace-building, conflict prevention, conflict resolution or peacemaking will be dealt with in later chapters. Here we shall focus very specifically on military intervention by a third party in armed conflict.

Perhaps the first thing to understand is that the only people who can resolve conflicts are the people who are involved in fighting and those who are affected by it. Those who 'own' the conflict must be those who 'own' the peace. So, and this will be another common thread running through almost everything from this chapter forward, as outsiders all we can do is help them towards that end.

Faced with public demands that 'something must be done', even the most powerful states and international organizations find themselves with limited options for intervention.

It is perhaps sensible first of all to tie down what we mean by intervention. In concentrating on military intervention by states, we will look at two particular types of activity: firstly, what the military call peace support operations and secondly, humanitarian intervention. Although, in practice, the dividing line between these two activities is very fuzzy, we will try to treat them separately, for reasons that I hope will become clear. Let it suffice to say for now that the first has been an accepted responsibility of the international community since 1945, while the second involves a much more controversial concept that, ironically, takes us back to the Just War ideas of the Middle Ages and beyond. As we look at a range of situations in the late twentieth century where these questions have come into focus, I hope we will be able to see the relevance of our Christian faith to reaching beyond the headlines.

Peace support operations

There are good reasons for focusing on the military first. Because they evoke the attention of the media, military peacekeeping or peace enforcement operations are the most obvious and visible forms of intervention. Together, these are usually known as peace support operations. Costly in terms of taxes and, more importantly, lives, they are frequently also controversial. There is often a long period of public and international debate leading up to deployment of a peacekeeping force, perhaps culminating in a United Nations Security Council Resolution. Even if such a resolution is passed, the lack of a standing United Nations force means that long delays can occur before any significant capability arrives on the scene.

For example, in the twelve months after United Nations Security Council Resolution 1769 was passed in July 2007, authorizing an increase of the international force in Darfur from about 7,000 to 24,000 military and police, the numbers barely topped 10,000. There are good reasons for this, including the remoteness of the location, the lack of any effective ceasefire, the need to cooperate with a sovereign Sudanese government and with a hotchpotch of rebel groups, and the lack of enthusiasm of potential donor nations to commit their own troops. Meanwhile, though, the plight of Darfurians worsened rather than improved, in contrast to the impression given of decisive action and the high expectations raised.

This is perhaps typical of the situation the United Nations has increasingly found itself in, as peacekeeping has developed from a relatively straightforward static 'holding the line' activity between forces that have agreed a ceasefire, such as in Cyprus, to something much more complicated. Today's peacekeeper is required to do much more, pushing the boundaries towards peace enforcement and beyond. Even if the mandate initially allowed by the Security Council is restrictive, the situation on the ground can easily force a change to a broader type of operation through 'mission creep'. Also, the intervening force can easily be drawn into the conflict, having been manipulated by one side or the other.

When we look at a situation like that of Somalia in 1992–94, it is frustrating to see that neither the most authoritative body in the world nor the most powerful nation in the world is in a position to bring such situations to a peaceful conclusion. Those who are interested in a detailed examination of the issues involved in current UN peacekeeping operations should look at the relatively up-to-date Brahimi Report, available from the United Nations website.[1] For our purposes here, though, we do not need to go into such detail.

This development of military peace support operations from straightforward neutral peacekeeping or even cease-fire observer operations into a much more complex set of demands is, of course, fraught with difficulties and ambiguities. Yet it is an inevitable consequence of the 'new wars' already described, and it is probably a much more realistic way of intervening in conflict than simply monitoring a ceasefire, with no attempt to unfreeze the conflict.

Policing of the 'Green Line' in Cyprus by the UN since 1974 has done little to resolve the conflict, which needed shifts in political attitudes on a much broader stage. However, it has arguably prevented armed conflict for three decades. Although examples of unintended and often disastrous consequences of armed intervention are legion, probably all but the most convinced pacifists would recognize situations where a robust armed presence can be a stabilizing factor in a civil war or other armed conflict. There are those who do not accept this, and we have to admire the courage of those who put their beliefs into practice, by travelling to dangerous conflict zones on peace missions. There is, of course, also a risk of unintended consequences of such peace interventions, and the possibility of putting others in danger.

However, this is not the main point here. Chapter 6 will suggest that the millions of pounds and thousands of lives invested in peacekeeping and peace enforcement are likely to be wasted if there is not also investment in the longer-term establishment and maintenance of peace. The soldiers will go home, for financial or other reasons, probably sooner than one might wish.

The need for sustained peace and stability is not controversial; most academics and decision-makers in this area agree with this point of view. Paddy Ashdown, for example, gives a pragmatic account of the various political elements that go into post-conflict 'stabilization'.[2] But that is a long way from putting it into action, and the focus of public debate often remains on military interventions. We will deal in more detail in later chapters with some of the alternatives and the biblical concepts that speak to these matters. For the moment, we need to recognize that peace means much more than just cessation of fighting. This is perhaps one area where a meeting of minds between Christian pacifists and other Christians might be especially helpful, so that they might make a contribution based on what they have in common.

Just War and peace support

Military peace support operations are an area where the Just War tradition is again an aid to clear thought about the ethics of a particular case, preferably in its more flexible and less systematized Augustinian form than the more legalistic later versions.

Looking first at how the soldier in the field operates in peace support operations, the problems are perhaps more subtle than those of a more conventional military operation, but fundamentally not very different from them. So the Just War ideas of *jus in bello* are very much applicable. As a reminder, there are two fundamental principles: proportionality in the use of force and discrimination of non-combatants from combatants. These are of course interconnected.

Most civil war situations are complex, messy and frustrating. Simply working out who is who is by no means simple. Just as with the War on Terror mentioned earlier, the protagonists do not wear uniforms and are not easily distinguishable from perfectly peaceful villagers, or, even more difficult, from civilians who are protesting against the presence of the foreigners in their land. Indeed, in asymmetric warfare (involving parties of dissimilar power) the weaker protagonist may well deliberately mingle with non-combatants in order to encourage attacks on civilians, both building indigenous solidarity against the foreign 'oppressor' and gaining an international public relations advantage. Without even considering the moral implications of overreacting to such provocations, the way the peacekeepers respond is going to have a critical effect on the success of the operation.

Although its prowess seems to have been overtaken by a quick-learning US military in the face of events in Iraq, the British Army has had a great deal of experience in this kind of warfare in Northern Ireland, and has been rightly seen as among the world's experts. I would not dream of putting forth my own ideas in the face of such experience. But it is worth noting how easily a good reputation can quickly be besmirched by incidents of torture or mistreatment of prisoners – clear breaches of the Just War tradition.

Turning to the question of going to war, there is a model for us here in the Old Testament, where the ability of the militia-based army of ancient Israel to go to war was highly dependent on broad support from the home front.[3] This placed a constraint on the ability of leaders to start a war. Similarly, we should as responsible Christian citizens examine our political leadership closely when decisions are made about committing troops. The *jus ad bellum* criteria make a helpful framework for doing so. The noble aim of restoring peace seems incontrovertible as a 'right intention'. However, there can be many hidden agendas as the political decisions are made, and the urgency of the need can hide aspects of the justice of the situation. An intervening military force may stop the fighting but inadvertently reinforce injustices that have developed.

The requirement to try to consider all alternatives before resorting to armed intervention is probably very likely to be met, not least because almost all such situations are referred to the 'right authority', generally accepted as the United Nations Security Council. Indeed, most states err on the reluctant side of intervention, and there is often very little appetite for committing troops when the national interest is not at stake. Then the Just War tradition's requirement for a 'reasonable probability of success', probably put in different terms and definitely without referring to Just War, can be used as an excuse to do nothing. There can be a form of racial prejudice here, with some lives being counted as of lower value than others. But the Christian has a very firm biblical mandate to assert that, in God's eyes, all humans are to be valued. And as we enter this kind of discussion we are starting to slip over that ill-defined boundary into interventions based on humanitarian concern.

Ultimately, we can do a lot worse than to keep our eyes focused on the quite recently added third element of the tradition: applying Just War to the 'end state' or *jus post bellum*. That will help us remember why we, or those who serve us, are there: namely to fulfil our responsibility to bring peace and stability to the victims of that particular conflict. Almost by definition, that will require us to look to the future righting of the wrongs that may have led to the violent conflict, something that is often beyond the scope and direct mandate of deployed military forces, but which the best of them are going to influence positively through the way they go about their tasks.

Humanitarian intervention

We recognized earlier in this chapter that it is difficult to draw a line between peacekeeping operations and humanitarian intervention, especially for soldiers in the field. However, it is a useful distinction for us to make as we move on to think about how the ideas surrounding humanitarian intervention developed.

Concepts of humanitarian intervention are not new. Augustine saw righting wrongs as a key reason to go to war and to override the rights of the sovereign government. Loosely translated, he wrote, 'In the absence of justice, what is sovereignty but organized robbery?' [4] His original concept of Just War, continued by Thomas Aquinas after him, included warfare to punish those 'princes' who transgress against natural law. Now this is of course a very dangerous path to tread. Knowing the history of the Crusades and of more modern forms of Holy War, we must be very cautious. However, in the concepts of 'Responsibility to Protect' espoused by the United Nations in 2005,[5] there is an unconscious and unwitting return to these older forms of the Just War tradition. In a sense, this is a return to Thomas More's ideas of what armies are for. In his book *Utopia*, he reports that the Utopians go to war only 'to protect their own land, to drive invading armies from the territories of their friends, or to liberate an oppressed people, in the name of humanity, from tyranny and servitude'.[6]

Now as then, there is a tension between human security or human rights, as we would say today, and the right of a legitimate government to sovereignty in its territory. For Christians this is a particularly relevant tension, because both concepts can be argued biblically. In the New Testament we read both of the requirement to respect government authorities and of the compassion of Jesus – to be emulated by us – for the poor and helpless.[7]

Arguably, humanitarian intervention was practised well before the twentieth century, although not by that name and in a very discriminatory way. Elements of humanitarian motivation were present when European powers intervened on several occasions during the nineteenth century to protect Christian subjects in Ottoman territory.[8] France intervened in 1842 to protect the Maronite Christians of Mount Lebanon, with Turkey's reluctant acquiescence. This highlights a further issue that resonates today, for example, in the acquiescence of the government of Sudan to the presence of African Union and United Nations troops in Darfur. There are ways of gaining 'consent' by threat or pressure. In these two nineteenth-century cases, the humanitarian motives were not to be dismissed, but nor were they particularly pure.

More recently, India claimed with some justification a humanitarian imperative for intervening in Bangladesh in 1971. However, Soviet attempts to justify the invasions of Hungary in 1956 and Czechoslovakia in 1968 on similar grounds remind us how easy and attractive it is to use such a justification, and show us the dangers of too easily sacrificing the principle of state sovereignty. So this debate is not new.

The classic case, of course, is the Holocaust, and the Western powers have been criticized for not doing more to stop the organized slaughter of the Jews and others. I remember being given a guided tour of the Yad Veshem Museum near Jerusalem and being challenged about the failure of

Allied bombers to cut the railway lines leading to extermination camps.

In 1939, international lawyer Ellery Stowell had already used the phrase 'humanitarian intervention'. He recognized the legal problems of pitting common standards of humanity against state sovereignty and concluded as follows.

> When, however, the conduct of a state, not excused by some untoward event like revolution or civil war, constitutes on the part of the responsible government a deliberate violation of that minimum of security and justice to which every individual in a civilised community is entitled, it becomes the right and the duty of other states to intervene in so far as is practicable to prevent or lessen such severities.[9]

I quote Stowell, little-known, at length, because he prefigures many of the current arguments about humanitarian intervention. At that time, a lot was known about the way the Nazis were maltreating Jews, although the Holocaust had not begun. In this quotation alone, we can see how the principles incorporated in the UN's 2005 'Responsibility to Protect' resolutions were already encapsulated. Recognition of the constraints of practicality was also included and reminds us of Just War's 'reasonable prospect of success'.

However, we can question whether humanitarian intervention really progressed beyond legal theory to practical action. That the USA did not intervene in Europe until itself attacked in December 1941 illustrates that the tension between humanitarian concerns and vital national interests was an issue then as now.

Regarding sovereignty, Jean Bethke Elshtain argues in a very complex theological-political-psychological work that our concept of sovereignty has shifted over the centuries away from the recognition of God's sovereignty, which formed the basis of the modern sovereign state, which itself then led to the postmodern concept of the sovereignty of the self.[10] No doubt this is an accurate picture of the development of human thought, and along the way she emphasizes some of the positive aspects of this development. But one of the foundations of the Christian faith is a proper understanding of God's continuing sovereignty throughout the ages.

Assessing whether there is a just cause for intervention might today seem to be very straightforward. Often there is a public outcry for action to stop the suffering, and rightly so. However, the information we receive through newspapers and the images we see on our television screens are unlikely to give us the full story. We all prefer a simple situation, with 'good guys' and 'bad guys'. In my experience, the real situation is always more complex and often very different from what is presented to us. For example, the complexities of the Kosovo situation, where subjugated Kosovo Albanians were freed from Serbian occupation, are with hindsight worthy of a more nuanced understanding. The Serbian minority in Kosovo are now in an unenviable position.

I have not seen the film *Black Hawk Down*, but the humiliating withdrawal of American troops from Somalia in the 1990s was a major setback to the concept of humanitarian intervention. There were those at that time who had high hopes of nurturing an emerging new norm: to intervene if a government failed to live up to its 'responsibility to protect' its citizens. They have continued to work towards it, if perhaps with a more realistic expectation. However, the US-led invasion of Iraq has seriously dented any appetite for humanitarian intervention. It is common even among moderates in the Middle East to say, either out of genuine concern or as a rhetorical weapon, 'We don't want Darfur to become another Iraq.' Champions of humanitarian intervention like Gareth Evans[11] argue that the use of humanitarian justifications to defend the invasion of Iraq has brought 'Responsibility to Protect' into disrepute. Particularly among Europeans, there has been reluctance to support the principle of humanitarian intervention for fear of tacitly legitimizing the invasion of Iraq.

But what does the Christian faith have to say about all of this?

Faced with the disadvantaging and even dehumanizing of ethnic groups, we must admit at least some obligation to try to correct the matter, despite the general biblical injunction to recognize and even obey the constituted government. But as always, the difficulty comes in the application. Are we responsible for righting wrongs anywhere in the world? There is a clear convention on genocide, but for a less extreme injustice, what constitutes a failure by a government to fulfil its responsibility? And is the military option always the answer?

Once again, the Just War tradition comes to our rescue. Or rather, elements of it do. Although out of fashion today, the need to enter conflict with a good intention speaks to the importance of motive, and helps us guard against the dangers of hubris and interventionism. The requirement to consider carefully the prospect of success of any operation keeps us from recklessness. Most of us would probably agree that we should think twice about invading China because of her human rights record. That is an extreme case, but some would argue against applying this sort of pragmatism to a matter of principle. I have to disagree, because we must always think twice about committing troops to a course of action where uncertainty is inevitable and some degree of unintended consequences very likely.

There are biblical aids to our thinking, too. As mentioned earlier, the advice by Jesus to 'offer to Caesar what is Caesar's and to God what is God's' sets the criterion by which victims of an unjust regime can test their duty to the state.

In deciding whether to act when we see injustice in the world, we are asking the perennial question: who is our neighbour? Perhaps the parable of the Good Samaritan told by Jesus helps us here.[12] It may not be the usual lesson we are supposed to learn from the parable, but we can note that the Samaritan helps the injured victim of robbers because he just happens to be passing by. He does not seek out the victim, but when the problem is brought to his attention, he does what he can. He does not try to do everything himself, either, but uses his wealth to leave behind some resources with the innkeeper so that the victim's needs are met in the longer term. Not all of us can deal with violent conflict directly, but most of us are blessed with financial and other resources that we can apply, often in a strategic way.

Also, in these days of mass communications, much more is brought to our attention than used to be the case, though sometimes with doubtful motives and accuracy. So our own situation is very different from someone simply walking along a road and discovering a victim. I do not think that we need to take responsibility for righting all of the wrongs in the world like Superman. It is enough for us to do what we can, when we can, where we can.

I do not think that we need to take responsibility for righting all of the wrongs in the world like Superman. It is enough for us to do what we can, when we can, where we can.

How is this relevant to the average Western Christian? Much of this chapter may seem to be quite abstract, and very remote from us sitting in our church pews. I wrote earlier of a sense of helplessness, and we may in particular think that all this military talk is nothing to do with us. However, I hope that the topics I have raised here will help us to understand a little more about the issues lying behind the headlines and the television news.

This chapter has been mostly about armed force. In the next chapter we will see that military power is not the be-all and end-all of dealing with conflict, and that, paradoxically, weakness has its place. I will progressively construct a bridge from this to the final chapters, leading us to a better understanding of the constructive non-military ways we can intervene in twenty-first-century conflict.

5 POWER AND WEAKNESS

'The strong do what they can and the weak suffer what they must.'
Thucydides, *The Peloponnesian War*, 89

'God is our refuge and strength, an ever-present help in trouble.
Therefore we will not fear, though the earth give way and the mountains
fall into the heart of the sea . . . "Be still, and know that I am God; I will
be exalted among the nations, I will be exalted in the earth."
The LORD Almighty is with us; the God of Jacob is our fortress.'
Psalm 46:1–2,10–11

What does it mean to be powerful?

We have seen in chapter 4 that armed force is the most visible, costly and controversial means of intervening in other people's wars. It is also in theory the way to apply the most political pressure and persuasion. Yet the 'Law of Unintended Consequences' can mean that the end result of our military intervention is far from what we wanted, expected or planned for. Examples roll off the tongue: Somalia, Kosovo, Iraq and the Falkland Islands. So although I do not subscribe to pacifism, I think we can be sure that military force is not always the most effective arrow in the quiver.

I hope here to link the rather topsy-turvy biblical view of power and weakness to modern concepts of power. I will suggest that hard power may be needed to restore stability, but is not necessarily effective in the long term. This will prepare the ground for looking at other types of intervention in the next chapter.

Gideon's story

It may seem inappropriate in a book that is mostly about peacemaking to use a military campaign to illustrate the contrast between power and weakness. However, the story of the military leader Gideon, as described in the book of Judges, seems to teach us many lessons. He was fighting a holy war, commanded by God, something that seems very alien to us today – and rightly so. We are not in the business of fighting holy wars, and we need to be very careful about imagining that God is on our side in battle, as Bob Dylan (something of a modern prophet) reminded us. Nevertheless, we have already seen that there are times when it is arguably right for us to fight in a just way, for a just cause.

As a former military planner, I could perhaps be expected to find the story of Gideon a strange narrative. But I suspect that *most* of us will find the story rather odd. Gideon is a very reluctant military commander, the least member of the weakest clan of Israel. He is reassured time and time again that God will give him victory against the Midianites, but he goes back to God time and time again to ask for a sign. . . and then another sign . . . and then another. Throughout all of this, God treats Gideon with patience, almost humouring him, until it is very clear to Gideon and to the reader that he is empowered by God for this special purpose.

Gideon then does what you or I might do. He sends out for as many men as he can get to join his army. But after they all arrive the Lord says to him, in my very loose translation, 'Hang on – that's too many', and tells Gideon to send home those who are afraid, about two-thirds of the number. So

now he is down to a volunteer army, but God demands a
further reduction to a force of 300, this time based on how
the soldiers drink, an even more bizarre concept. One might
argue that those who stayed on their feet and lapped water
out of their hands were being more wary, alert and therefore
soldier-like than those who got down on their knees and
drank directly from the pool. Or one could say that the test
was totally arbitrary. I am not sure that it matters either way.
The main point is that Gideon and his people were supposed
to recognize their dependence on God for this victory, and
not to think it was won through their own strength.

Ultimately, Gideon trusts God, especially after he has been
given an opportunity to listen in to the conversations of the
Midianites. Informed by a dream, they are beginning to be
fearful that they are bound to be defeated by Gideon.

However, Gideon still has a problem. Empowered as he is by
the Holy Spirit, reassured as he is that the battle is all but won
before it has even started, he still has to work out how he will
use his puny force of 300 to defeat a force perhaps ten or twenty
times as large. It is a reminder to us that depending on God does
not at all mean just sitting back and waiting for a miracle to
sort the problem out. Indeed, Gideon does not just sit back. He
resorts to what today would be called psychological warfare,
by getting his 300 men to make plenty of noise with their trum-
pets and voices, and by using lights to give the appearance of
surrounding the Midianite camp. As a result, chaos and panic
ensue, with the Midianites fighting among themselves in the
confusion of the night, and eventually being routed.

So Gideon, who had been told 'Go in the strength you
have', eventually, after several attempts to do otherwise,
depended on God, and weakness won the day over superior
strength.

What are the lessons in this story? One, borne out by

military history, is that some of the best military commanders are those with a sense of humility and even of their
dependence on God. This is not an image of the military that
strikes a chord with some, although there are instances. Two
British examples are the operational exploits of General Bill
Slim in Burma in 1943–45 and the capture of Goose Green by
2nd Battalion, the Parachute Regiment during the Falklands
War.[1] There is also a good precedent for this in the centurion
who trusted Jesus for the healing of his servant.[2]

Also, if we approach whatever tasks we have been given
with an attitude of pride and self-importance, we can expect
quite soon to be deflated – and not necessarily treated with
the patience and long-suffering that Gideon was shown.
But the main lesson for the purposes of this chapter is that,
in God's economy, power and strength are not necessarily
measured in battalions and tanks.

Power and twenty-first-century wars

It is indisputable that power relationships play an important
role in the 'new wars' described in chapter 1. However, this is
the case in two quite distinct but interconnected ways: within
the conflict situation itself and with respect to third parties
who may think of intervening.

Intra-state conflict is very likely to involve parties of dissimilar power. Indeed, the attempt to correct this imbalance
may be a cause of the violence, and this will in turn affect the
way the conflict is played out, leading to what is known as
asymmetric warfare. Asymmetry will force the weaker party
to use indirect means to challenge the stronger; these may
include hit-and-run tactics, terrorism and sabotage. Indeed,
armed groups fighting a government may use tactics that are
expressly aimed at provoking an overreaction so as to exploit
international public opinion on the side of the underdog.

Couple this with the fact that these weaker armed groups
are likely to be irregular, to be poorly equipped and to have
limited resources, and we end up with several consequences.
For example, their tactics are unlikely to be constrained
by international norms or rules of warfare – the *jus in bello*
described earlier – possibly inciting the stronger party to
respond in kind. Internationally, weaker parties may use
diaspora connections, the printed and visual media, the
Internet and international public opinion networks to further
their cause. If they are successful in putting over this propaganda more effectively than the stronger party's propaganda,
they can gain sympathy that is more powerful than tanks. We
who read in our Bibles of God's bias towards the side of the
poor and oppressed, and who do not know enough about the
situation to discern which message is right, are perhaps most
likely to jump to premature conclusions.

Also, these armed groups may not have any sources of
income, food or weapons, so they may need to seek economic
and other support from the local populace. This could be
by persuasion or coercion, adding to the impact on civilians
that I mentioned earlier. Or they may turn to neighbouring
regimes and gain their support and refuge in their territory by
making common cause with them politically. Then the likeli-
hood increases that regional and other international powers
or transnational agencies will become embroiled in the conflict. For example, Sudan's long-running civil wars since the
1950s have been made much more complex by the involvement from time to time of other states in the region, many
of which have supported or hosted Sudanese rebel groups.
Sudan has in turn backed groups rebelling against neighbouring regimes, such as the Lord's Resistance Army in Uganda.

The other way in which power relationships enter the
equation relates to third parties that intervene, often with

admirable intentions. In practice, those who apparently hold overwhelming economic, military and political power in the world may be unable to make any effective intervention in these complex internal conflicts. Recent history is full of examples where, even when public opinion clamoured that 'something must be done', the most powerful nations in the world seemed not just unwilling but even unable to take appropriate action. Take Somalia, where ruthless warlords, backed up by what became known as the 'CNN effect' that brings the suffering and humiliation of 'our boys' to family television screens, triggered the withdrawal of US forces and severely affected the way intervention policy developed in the following years. The link is clear between the Somalia experience and international failure or inability to stop genocide in Rwanda soon afterwards. And as we saw when thinking about the Global War on Terror, military power used inappropriately can have unintended consequences that make it counter-productive.

Commentators on international politics have recognized this, of course, and there have been calls, for instance, consistently by Joseph Nye, for the USA to make more effective and cleverer use of her 'soft power'.[3] Even at the height of the USA's post-Cold War status as the world's 'undisputed global hegemony', Nye was arguing that military power is not enough, and warning against arrogance and triumphalism. He wrote of the 'paradox of American power', suggesting in the context of the War on Terror that the strongest nation in the world could not get what it wants without the cooperation of other less powerful states. As well as emphasizing the principles of multilateralism, Nye suggests that American power is not, or should not be, just measured in military spending and capability, but also in attitudes, in ephemeral assets like popularity and attractiveness. For the USA, this requires not only an investment in public diplomacy, with the dangers of resorting to propaganda, but also the need to listen to the rest of the world. Nye's message fell on very sceptical ears for much of the George W. Bush presidency, but Barack Obama and his administration seem to see the point.

Readers of the Bible perhaps instinctively understand this, having heard of Goliath being defeated by a young shepherd boy with a slingshot, Samson being robbed of his strength by a woman and a barber, and the story of Gideon recounted above.

The power of non-violence

These examples bring us to a place where principles of non-violent resistance of evil or oppression are on their strongest ground. Basing their approach on Jesus' saying, 'Do not resist an evil person. If someone strikes you on the right cheek, turn to him the other also'[4], they argue for the moral strength of non-violence. Of course, Jesus on the cross is a supreme example of acceptance of violence, but, except perhaps in this very special case, proponents of non-violent engagement like John Howard Yoder and Martin Luther King argue against this kind of apparent passivity, proposing instead active non-violent opposition.[5] In fact, the impression we gain of the demeanour of Jesus from the Passion narratives paradoxically shows a person in full control, despite his apparent helplessness.

Those who espouse non-violent resistance have some strong evidence available. In the particular case of resistance to a repressive government, Maria Stephan and Erica Chenoweth have recently published research that provides powerful arguments for the effectiveness of non-violent action instead of armed revolution. They cite Serbia in 2000, Madagascar in 2002, Georgia in 2003, the Ukraine in 2004–5,

Lebanon in 2005 and Nepal in 2006 as places where 'organized civilian populations successfully employed non-violent
methods including boycotts, strikes, protests, and organized non-cooperation to challenge entrenched power and
exact political concessions'.[6] Their statistical research shows
twice as many successful outcomes from non-violent as
from violent resistance. They also suggest that non-violent
popular resistance movements are more likely than violent
rebellions to be successful in the face of repression, to enjoy
international sympathy and to lead to a successful negotiated
outcome.

These findings make a lot of sense. The reasons are intui-
tively clear: non-violent resistance increases domestic and
international legitimacy, encourages the broadening of the
movement, and makes it more difficult for a regime to react
violently without a popular backlash and a negative reaction
from outside the country. Even the most repressive leaders
need loyal functionaries to 'do their dirty work'. That loyalty
is likely to be much less solid, and will extend to a much
smaller number of supporters, if they are faced with a non-
violent movement with mass support than with a group of
armed – even well-armed – guerrillas whose motivations are
unclear and whose domestic support base is less extensive.

One example of a successful non-violent campaign is the
toppling of Philippine President Ferdinand Marcos in 1986
by a pro-democracy movement. Stephan and Chenoweth
describe how 'a broad-based coalition of opposition politicians, workers, students, businesspeople, Catholic Church
leaders, and others non-violently coerced a regime whose
legitimacy was already weakening', despite widely held
expectations of a violent overthrow. Armed Communist
resistance movements existed. But it was the angry national
and international reaction to the assassination of the most

prominent opposition leader, Benigno Aquino, as he returned from exile in 1983, which started the process leading to Marcos's downfall.

Following elections stolen by Marcos in early 1986, Corazón (Cory) Aquino, the widow of Benigno, led a mass movement of non-violent protest and boycotts targeting the corrupt media, banks and businesses. Military repression backfired as the US withdrew its support of Marcos and 'helped' him to leave the country. Cory Aquino became President. During the process, a movement for reform of the armed forces had grown into large-scale defections. Also, the churches had played a significant role on behalf of the non-violent campaign and helped to keep support away from the Communist guerrillas. In this, as in other cases described in the research, the authors show that violent opposition movements are much less likely to gain domestic support and the crucial international sympathy enjoyed by non-violent mass campaigns.

Thus it seems clear that there are situations where the non-violent approach is more effective. Of course, pacifist proponents of a non-violent approach might say that this is a much too pragmatic way of looking at the issue. Non-violence is simply right. Viewed pragmatically, though, the superiority of non-violence seen in cases of resistance to oppression does not necessarily apply to other situations. There are many cases, in my view, where the robust use of military force can lead to a better outcome for the victims of oppression, and is indeed the right thing to do. The Second World War seems a clear example of this, even though many evils were perpetrated on both sides.

However, these are questions already dealt with in chapter 2. The key issue here is an insidious temptation that we all face: to rely on our own strength. We read in Psalm 20 and

also in more or less the same terms from Isaiah, 'Some trust
in chariots and some in horses, but we trust in the name of
the LORD our God.' [7] This, it seems, is the message of Jesus,
both when he praises the Roman officer's faith and when he
tells Peter to put up his sword. Indeed, this is the message of
the whole Bible on this question.

There is a mystery here, linking
power, weakness, sovereignty and
faith. It is captured by Dietrich
Bonhoeffer in his 'Articles of Faith on
the Sovereignty of God in History':

> *There is a mystery
> here, linking power,
> weakness, sovereignty
> and faith.*

> I believe that God can and will bring good out of evil. For that
> purpose he needs men who make the best use of everything.
> I believe God will give us all the power we need to resist in all
> times of distress. But he never gives it in advance, lest we should
> rely upon ourselves and not on him alone. [8]

This contrast between power and weakness reaches a poignant level in the city of Jerusalem, the focal point of one of
the most intractable violent conflicts of our day.

Power at Golgotha

A couple of years ago, I boarded a bus in east Jerusalem, just
outside the Damascus Gate, to travel to Bethlehem.

The Bethlehem bus does not go to Bethlehem. It goes
only as far as the 'separation fence' or 'wall' (the description
depends on whether you talk to Israelis or Palestinians), [9]
where passengers alight and continue on foot through the
checkpoint, responding to gestured commands from Israeli
soldiers seated behind blast-proof glass. On the other side,
taxis provide the link for the short remaining distance.

As we approached the checkpoint, the faces of my

Palestinian fellow-passengers showed sullen resignation. The eight-metre concrete slabs of the wall are covered in angry graffiti, directly or satirically demanding the removal of the barrier. Israelis retort that the barrier has vastly reduced the ability of suicide bombers to pose a threat in Israel. In Bethlehem, Palestinian traders complain about their impoverishment through the collapse of the tourist trade.

The bus station in east Jerusalem is a curious place. At the back of the open area where buses arrive, park and depart stands a rocky escarpment, like a cliff. It is not high or in any way impressive, but many see in it the shape of a skull. This site was apparently associated with the prophet Jeremiah as the place where he lamented over Jerusalem, and known by Sephardic Jews as the 'place of stoning', an execution ground. Archaeological evidence and biblical interpretation during the nineteenth century progressively convinced some British Protestants that this hill, not the traditional site in the centre of the city on which the Church of the Holy Sepulchre had been constructed, was Golgotha, the site of Jesus' crucifixion. Prominent among those who believed this was General Charles Gordon, who spent a year in Palestine shortly before his death. I have often passed the site in Khartoum where he was killed.

Close by the Jerusalem bus station, in sight of the escarpment, is a garden where a tomb has been excavated, hewn from the rock and believed by some to be the one donated by Joseph of Arimathea for Jesus to be laid in. This garden is a special place at any time, but particularly at Easter. While I was writing this chapter, my wife and I found ourselves on Easter Day 2009 in noisy, bustling Venice and sought out the calm of St George's Anglican Church, in a former glass warehouse facing the Grand Canal. As I enjoyed the Easter worship and listened to the last sentences of the Gospel of

Mark, I recalled visits to the tranquil garden in Jerusalem. Unlike the crowded Church of the Holy Sepulchre, beset for centuries by internecine squabbles that left different areas of the church in the hands of different denominations, the garden is a peaceful place close to the heart of a city in conflict. Few visit it. Whatever the truth of the competing claims of the different sites, the Garden Tomb gives me a greater sense of the reality of the crucifixion and the resurrection than does the Holy Sepulchre.

There is a more profound point than my impressions of Jerusalem, which elevates the question of power and weakness to the cosmic level. We see, in the acceptance by Jesus of his execution on the cross, not just the ultimate sacrifice. At the heart of the Christian faith is the belief that, by this supreme act of submission and apparent weakness, the three-in-one God performed the most powerful act of history.

Weak equals strong

We finish this chapter on power with the apostle Paul describing in his second letter to the Corinthian church how he asked God to remove the weakness or disability that he saw as constraining his ability:

> But he said to me, 'My grace is sufficient for you, for my power is made perfect in weakness.' Therefore I will boast all the more gladly about my weaknesses, so that Christ's power may rest on me. That is why, for Christ's sake, I delight in weaknesses, in insults, in hardships, in persecutions, in difficulties. For when I am weak, then I am strong.[10]

This is God's wisdom, the apparently inverted logic of the Bible that we also read about in Paul's first letter to the Christians at Corinth.[11]

It may be very difficult for those who appear, to others and themselves, to wield awesome power, to accept that their power has bounds. It has been my experience that those individuals who are given responsibility to bring resolution to civil wars, with military force or diplomatic muscle, find it very difficult to accept that others with fewer resources and less influence and power can play a useful role.

We will start to deal with this perception in the next chapter when we cover the range of conflict interventions. Other forms of engagement than military power are needed, and we will spend a little time looking both at the timing of any conflict intervention and at the different levels of society and forms of activity that may be needed to establish lasting peace and stability.

6 INTERVENING IN ARMED CONFLICT – THE NON-MILITARY WAY

'Blessed are the peacemakers, for they will be called sons of God.'
Matthew 5:9

It sounds so simple and straightforward: 'Blessed are the peacemakers.'

When at the start of this book we looked at the mostly intra-state conflict often called 'new wars', we noted several characteristics: the impact on civilians; the effects of globalization and fragmentation; and the apparent intractability of violent competition over power, resources and identity within a state. The question for this chapter, as for the preceding two, is: with all of these complications, should outsiders intervene, and if so, how? What does it mean to be a peacemaker?

We have recognized that those involved in fighting, or affected by it, 'own' the conflict, so the role of outsiders is to help them towards the peace that they must also 'own'. We dealt specifically with military intervention, the most obvious, the most powerful and the most costly form of intervention, and left the many other forms of third-party involvement – the weaker ones – for here. We recognized how sceptically the weak can be viewed, but also how deceptive power can be. So this chapter is only peripherally about power and weakness. The aim here is to argue for third-party involvement in armed conflict that is comprehensive in every sense, and specifically in ways that answer two questions: how and when?

Demands for military intervention in a conflict situation, often triggered by political pressure in the face of existing or impending humanitarian catastrophe, are generally urgent and reach the decision-makers at a late stage in a crisis. So those with the responsibility to decide what to do are often trying to catch up with unfolding events. They are rarely able to respond quickly enough or to do more than put a lid on the unfolding situation at best. Actions taken in a crisis are rarely sufficient or comprehensive enough, and can generally do little to deal with the underlying issues or causes. There has been a growing recognition in the United Nations and elsewhere of the importance of peace-building – that is, dealing with issues such as governance, equity and reconciliation – as well as peacekeeping. The United Nations Peacebuilding Commission was established in December 2005, but placed the peace-building responsibility of the UN firmly in the post-conflict context, and in general excluded any attempt to engage in preventive peace-building where a UN peacekeeping presence was not already in place. In its first years, the Commission was authorized to focus on post-conflict Burundi and Sierra Leone, but later started to look at other countries.

Yet the UN is not the only organization that can play a part in preventing or resolving intra-state conflict. Indeed, it has some disadvantages. Its intervention can be blocked by the veto of a permanent member of the Security Council and, even if intervention is authorized, the time between decision and effective action can be long. Other organizations, less powerful but more flexible and significantly less expensive, may sometimes be more effective or supplement the UN's efforts.

Not only is action needed on a broader front; it is needed earlier. As well as official scepticism about the overall role of those involved unofficially in dealing with violent conflict, there are also doubts about the ability of the 'small fry' to deliver the goods the international community thinks it needs, when it needs them. This is primarily about time horizons, which is my point of departure for this chapter.

When is the right time?

The concentration on military intervention by the UN, a 'coalition of the willing' or a regional entity can be counterproductive, not least because it can lead to the assumption of a fixed sequence of actions. This starts when the international community perceives a challenge to peace and perhaps attempts preventive diplomacy, leading to a peacekeeping or peace-enforcement operation, followed by a period of post-conflict peace-building. There may be a successful attempt to persuade the warring parties to sign a peace accord. Sadly, though, this neat sequence is rarely realistic. It is by definition a failure of preventive diplomacy that causes a military peacekeeping intervention or a mediation attempt. The case for at least trying prevention is powerfully argued by Michael Lund, who also describes the wide range of official and unofficial forms such action may take.[1] So we will first take a brief look at prevention, of which preventive diplomacy is the central activity.

Preventive diplomacy is almost by definition an ad hoc activity demanding flexibility and creativity. In theory, the well-resourced, diplomatically privileged officials of states or international organizations are best placed to undertake this activity. But preventive diplomacy cannot operate in a vacuum; it must depend on existing relationships and long-term knowledge of a particular situation for its success.

Perhaps for these reasons, some argue that the international record of preventive diplomacy in recent years has not been strong. For example, William Zartman of Johns Hopkins University suggests that international diplomatic intervention in Yugoslavia in the winter of 1989–90 might have pre-empted the collapse of the federation.[2] Thinking about such 'alternate realities' is not easy, but the cost in lives and money of almost a decade of civil war must make such attempts worth the effort.

If we accept that it is worth investing in prevention, then the question of who does it becomes even more important. The accepted wisdom, that this lies with international agencies like the United Nations or diplomats of interested countries, is not enough. As we will see in the next chapter, there are organizations that invest time and effort over years in conflict areas, which do not carry with them the baggage of national interest or the potential to be accused of neo-imperialism. Given the resources, they have potential to make a much greater contribution to prevention than they are currently asked to do.

Zartman has also written extensively about the 'ripeness' of conflict for resolution and refers to a time when a 'hurting stalemate' causes the parties to see negotiation as a better strategic option than continuing to fight. Yet even he recognizes that this can be too simplistic – that we do not necessarily need to be passive. We may be able to create ripeness rather than just wait for it to turn up. Or there may be multiple ripe moments, so that – like buses – missing one does not necessarily mean we have lost the opportunity. In any case, it is hard to see how to predict ripeness in advance – it is much easier to recognize after the fact.

So the timing of intervention matters. A military peacekeeping operation may well be needed to re-establish some

element of stability and civilian protection, but this will often
be a very late response after lives have been lost and positions
have hardened. Secondly, although the benefits of some kind
of preventive diplomacy are clear, the focus by diplomats on
short-term goals and crisis management may make it difficult
for them to provide what is needed: continuous long-term
involvement.

Often there is real urgency in dealing with the immediate humanitarian crisis, as horrific events are brought to our
notice. Yet time is needed to deal properly with hatred and
bitterness. Also, to return to the theme of topsy-turvy logic,
we read, 'But do not forget this one thing, dear friends: With
the Lord a day is like a thousand years, and a thousand years
are like a day.'[3]

If the conflict has already broken out and it is too late for
preventive diplomacy, a military peacekeeping operation
may be needed. Alongside it, though, there will have to be
some form of mediation.

Mediation

Where violent conflict has already broken out, whether or
not a peacekeeping operation is in place, preventive diplomacy (if any) has failed and mediation of a peace agreement
will be necessary. Theories of mediation that have been
developed over preceding decades are not necessarily ade-
quate for the complexities of post-Cold War conflict.

Laurie Nathan summarizes a helpful set of six strategic
principles for mediation in intra-state crises. He suggests
that:

- mediators should not be partisan
- the parties must consent to mediation and the choice of
  the mediator

- all have to recognize that conflict cannot be resolved quickly and easily
- the parties must own the settlement
- mediators should not apply punitive measures
- mediation is a specialized activity.

None of this is particularly surprising, but Nathan's compilation of principles is helpful. He has also commented on the well-resourced but ultimately unsuccessful official Abuja talks, which in 2005–6 tried to settle the complex conflict in Darfur and for which these principles were not followed.[4]

While we consider mediation and before we move on to the broader range of interventions, let's look at the ideas of Thomas Princen about intermediaries, which I find quite helpful. Princen distinguishes between two types of intermediary: the 'principal mediator', which becomes involved in mediation because it has interests in the dispute and its resolution, and the 'neutral mediator', whose only interest in the dispute is that it be resolved.[5] Also, it is likely that the first has power and influence: the USA in the Middle East would be an example. The second, probably a non-official, has no means of applying sanctions to the parties and an example might be a church body. According to Princen, the first type encourages separate negotiation by the parties with the intermediary over incentives and payoffs, while the second encourages direct engagement between the two or more parties involved in the dispute. It is not that one is better than the other, rather that each has different strengths, but I would suggest that the genuinely neutral intermediary – probably holding no official authority – has a real role to play.

Non-governmental mediators may not be able to reward or coerce the parties, but one of their greatest strengths is likely to be their expertise and knowledge, born of their determination and ability to invest time and effort in the conflict over an extended period. This is where individuals and organizations pursuing an approach born of Christian values can be especially effective, not only in direct mediation, but in the much broader range of activities we will now move on to examine. The longer-term perspective needed to achieve sustainable peace in the complex conflicts described – moving beyond simple mediation aimed at getting a peace settlement signed – can contribute to conflict prevention, peacemaking and peace-building in a variety of different ways that can complement the efforts of officials. It is here that the broader range of organizations and individuals have a role to play.

Who are the peacemakers?

There are hundreds of organizations working in different ways on conflict, with different approaches that might be frustrating for those who like neatness and consistency. Here we will focus on organizations either with an explicit Christian outlook or whose methodology is in some way derived from Christian principles. This is not to ignore the excellent work being done by other organizations, and I have learned a great deal during the past five years from those whose commitment to conflict prevention, conflict resolution and peace-building comes from some other religious background or from an entirely secular viewpoint. I suspect that the religious / secular divide is not where the greater differences arise. It is perhaps fair to say that the greater division within the conflict resolution field is a sort of crisis of identity, for individuals and organizations, as to whether they are part of a principled 'peace movement' or take a more pragmatic approach.

Those who are committed to campaigning for peace are often just as committed to human rights issues, and may face a dilemma, in that advocacy for human rights does not necessarily lead to a peaceful resolution of differences. We will return to this apparent contradiction between peace and justice later.

The aspects of peace advocacy that strike our consciousness most directly are public demonstrations and newspaper advertising, protesting against this or that aspect of public policy, such as the invasion of Iraq. Although such demonstrations can make the participants feel that they have done something for peace and/or for human rights, they do tend to focus on one issue without necessarily recognizing some of the complexities laid out in earlier chapters of this book. It is, in my view, sometimes questionable whether their overall impact leads to greater stability or to peaceful outcomes. Among the most committed of the activists for peace are those who put their beliefs into practice by 'deploying' into conflict zones, performing tasks like accompanying Palestinians across the Israeli security wall. Many take as their model non-violent civil rights activists like Martin Luther King.

Another form of Christian involvement in armed conflict, which we would not naturally consider in this context, is the military chaplain, who does not necessarily fit the caricature of 'blessing the guns'. I recall talking to one very impressive chaplain to the Royal Marines who had completed the full Marine training course alongside the fighting men, and was therefore able to hold their respect and help them gain perspective as he preached to them on 'love your enemies' in the terrifying situations they faced in Afghanistan and Iraq.

Somewhere between these extremes is a whole range of types of work. The next chapter will deal in more detail with the pragmatic unofficial diplomacy with which I have become familiar in the past six years. First, though, I need to explain the framework that forms the context for this work, and the many other types of activity that can be called peacemaking.

Peace and justice

We've looked at timing, considering a range of activities stretching along what is called the conflict cycle and suggesting the need for comprehensiveness in terms of chronology. However, there are other ways in which we need a comprehensive approach: specifically in terms of types of activity and of levels of society.

The so-called 'intractable' conflicts are not amenable to resolution by mere negotiations, but need attention to the underlying inequalities and injustices in society. So preventive diplomacy, military peacekeeping operations or mediation, while they may provide a temporary settlement, are unlikely to lead to sustained stability. The question then is this: how is sustained peace to be achieved?

The foundation of the answer to this question, as helpfully laid out by Jeremy Ive and others, lies in the creative tension between peace (Hebrew *šālôm*) and justice (*ṣedeq* or *mišpāṭ*).[6] Without peace, justice cannot prevail over lawlessness. Without justice, peace cannot be sustained in the long term.

We learn from the Bible that peace – whether we speak of *šālôm* in Hebrew, *eirēnē* in Greek or *salaam* in Arabic – is much more than the cessation of hostilities, however essential that may be as a first step. Within the word are contained concepts of wholeness, integrity, well-being, health, healing, peace, completeness and welfare that the

We learn from the Bible that peace – whether we speak of šālôm in Hebrew, eirēnē in Greek or salaam in Arabic – is much more than the cessation of hostilities, however essential that may be as a first step.

English word does not come close to capturing, whether applied to individuals or, more appropriately, to communities.

This has three implications for a society in conflict: the need for comprehensive peacemaking in terms of levels of society; the need for comprehensive peacemaking in terms of types of activity; and the need to recognize that this can not be done overnight. Ultimately, as we shall see later, the goal is to achieve reconciliation, but this is in a sense the final step in a process, and it may be years, decades or even generations in coming. And to link this point to earlier chapters, it seems very difficult for anyone to sustain peacemaking activity in the long term, in the face of disappointment, opposition, disillusionment and lack of resources, without at least some degree of hope founded on the sovereignty of God.

Top, bottom, middle

One of the recognized experts in the field, John Paul Lederach, who comes from a Mennonite tradition, has something to say about levels of society. He suggests that peacemaking needs to go on at three 'levels of leadership', namely the political leadership, the grassroots communities and a third group of senior 'mid-range' leaders who are linked with their political leaders and hold respect at the grassroots.[7] As we will see in more detail in the next chapter, the organization I have the privilege to lead, Concordis International, focuses on this third influential group, with the aim that they will influence the levels above and below them. However, Lederach's point is that all three levels need attention. There are organizations working at the other two levels, of course.

One Christian organization working at the grassroots is the Christian International Peace Service, known rather deliciously as CHIPS, which has a distinguished history of over forty years of work in Cyprus and in northern Uganda. CHIPS sends teams of Christian volunteers to live among the local people and to undertake very practical development projects involving people from all sides of the conflict. The whole is backed up by work to break down barriers and by prayer. This is a very practical example of the holistic approach I have been suggesting, where concern for the physical needs of the community goes hand in hand with involvement in issues of justice and fairness. And of course CHIPS is focusing on peace in the broader sense of *šālôm*.

The level of peacemaking that gains the most attention – in the media, in academic analysis and by political leaders – is of course that involving political leaders. The efforts to reach a political settlement between warring parties, whether by the Secretary-General of the United Nations, diplomats of major world powers or senior 'private citizens' who are ex-presidents or ex-prime ministers, are hounded assiduously by international press and television. Sometimes, non-officials have assisted and supported mediators on a consultancy basis, but it is actually quite unusual for an unofficial organization, especially a Christian one, to be entrusted with mediating a political settlement itself. One rare exception is the case of Mozambique, where international recognition of the Community of Sant'Egidio's existing relationships led to Italy, other states and the United Nations offering logistic and political support for direct mediation by Sant'Egidio of a settlement between the Mozambiquan government and rebels in 1992.

However, a political settlement is just one of the elements of peacemaking on the long road to sustainable peace – towards *šālôm*. So, having looked at levels of society, we will move on to the other dimension of the comprehensiveness mentioned earlier: the need for a variety of activities to be working in concert.

From every angle

Some of the elements that are needed alongside a political settlement have already come up in earlier chapters. However, let's draw them all together here, with a few brief comments on each one. The assumption, for example, in the United Nations, is generally that these activities are needed in a post-conflict phase as part of a neatly planned sequence, but I hope it will be very obvious that this work is important at any time.

There are many different ways of looking at this question of comprehensiveness, but the main point is that many things need to be going on at once. In no particular order of importance, one can identify at least seven areas of activity that all need to be happening in concert in order to build sustainable peace, or *šālôm*, which are:

- the need to stabilize the military situation
- the disarmament, demobilization and reintegration of combatants
- the control of small arms and light weapons
- community-level peace-building
- the reconstruction of homes, agriculture and a legitimate economy
- post-conflict justice and reconciliation
- policy dialogue.

The first and most obvious is the need to stabilize the military situation, through agreeing and monitoring realistic ceasefires: separating forces, agreeing buffer zones and zones of control, setting up confidence-building measures and so forth. These are crucial but relatively technical military procedures that can be carried out robustly and with fairness by well-trained military forces, among whom we can definitely count the British Army. These actions need to form part of a comprehensive peace settlement, but often, in the rush to get a signed agreement by some particular deadline, the expertise needed to plan this in detail is not called on or properly consulted. This was the case in the N'Djamena and Abuja negotiations over the Darfur conflict, according to Jeremy Brickhill, who was one of the security experts concerned.[8] Unrealistic mediation often treats security arrangements as an add-on to a so-called comprehensive political settlement.

The second aspect, also focused on the security area, is the disarmament, demobilization and reintegration of former combatants, known as DDR, the first of many acronyms that trip lightly off the tongue and conceal the complexity of what lies behind them. It seems to me that the military and the international agencies are very good at disarmament and demobilization, but there is often a vacuum in capability when it comes to reintegration, the most difficult element. There are no easy answers here, but it can not suffice simply to remove weapons from militias and place them in camps awaiting some kind of vaguely planned retraining. A recipe for violent chaos! The reintegration perhaps needs to be in place first, before anyone considers disarming those who have been fighting.

This leads on to the third aspect, the control of small arms and light weapons, or SALW. Again, this is a very difficult factor in helping societies to return from civil war to peace. These may be societies where possession of a weapon is part of the culture, the key to protection of family and even an essential part of manhood. With the widespread and cheap availability of powerful weapons like Kalashnikov assault rifles, the stakes are raised. Inter-family or inter-clan disputes over real or imagined injuries are much more likely to escalate beyond the ability of the traditional authorities if the weapons used are capable of killing large numbers of people. Solutions to these problems probably need to be found at a global level. Processes brought by well-meaning international agencies into a local environment can easily have unintended consequences. Weapons bought up to take them out of circulation, for instance, can easily be replaced from elsewhere, boosting a lucrative trade in arms.

The fourth aspect is the whole area of community-level peace-building, which often builds on traditional methods of dispute resolution that go back centuries. What are the best ways to support these peacemaking processes, or to return them to their former strength? There must be many ways to do this, but one thing is certain: it will be essential to understand how the society works, and this can not be achieved in a short deployment of months or even a year or two. This brings us back to the need mentioned above for long-term engagement, throughout the so-called conflict cycle. This sustained commitment is exemplified by the CHIPS model described above.

Conflict, by definition, leaves behind it a trail of destruction. Not only are people killed, and homes and property destroyed. The means of livelihood are taken out of the reach of families whose grip on survival was probably already quite precarious. Many will have lost members of their families. Many are forced from their homes and end up living in camps, dependent on handouts from the World Food Programme, building a culture of dependency that can last decades. So the fifth element of my list is the massively costly process of reconstructing homes, rebuilding agriculture and reinvigorating a legitimate economy. If this process does not take place, refugees and the internally displaced will not dare to return to the home areas, even if their basic security needs have been met.

The sixth aspect is the whole area of post-conflict justice

and reconciliation, following periods when neighbours have turned against neighbours, and terrible atrocities may have been committed. We might call this 'dealing with the past'. It is a difficult and sensitive area to which there are no simple or universal answers. Chapter 8 will deal with this in much more depth.

These first six aspects need a whole range of skills and capabilities, some requiring official 'clout', others a more subtle unofficial approach. Most importantly, like oarsmen, they need to be pulling together in the same direction. This may mean that some overarching authority should coordinate all of the efforts, and the United Nations has often tried to fulfil this role in a post-conflict environment. However, as we have seen above, dealing with the conflict after it has happened is not enough. Even in the post-conflict scenario, non-governmental organizations, NGOs, are not very amenable to being coordinated, and the authority of the United Nations over them is at best doubtful. Most importantly, this kind of coordination leads us into the trap of instrumentalism, the idea that 'we', the outsiders, know what is best for 'them', the actors and victims in the conflict. This is far from recognizing that the ownership of the conflict and its solutions belong to the people involved.

So this is one of the roles of the seventh aspect on my list, which I have called policy dialogue, encouraging the changes in policies and practices that may have led to the conflict in the first place – the inequalities, the unfairness, the failures of governance and other underlying causes of these so-called intractable conflicts. This is where genuine engagement between policy-makers and others who can influence policy is an essential part of the picture. Such is the purpose of Concordis International and the area on which we will concentrate in the next chapter.

'It is well to remember, my son, that the entire population of the universe, with one trifling exception, is composed of others.' John Andrew Holmes, *Wisdom in Small Doses*

'Time is the currency of relationships.' Michael Schluter

Darfur

We may think we know all about Darfur. Perhaps some of us have marched along Whitehall in London or to the White House in protest against what has been going on there. Yet for most, the engagement stops there, and few could genuinely claim to understand the problem.

Darfur, the western region of Sudan and the 'land of the Fur', the largest tribe in the region, was a proudly independent sultanate that was left relatively untouched by the outside world even during the colonial period, until annexed to Anglo-Egyptian Sudan in 1916 for reasons of Great Power politics. Although there had previously been conflict in the region, the current civil war in Darfur started in February 2003 with an attack by Darfurian rebels on a government military base in Golu, followed up by a number of military successes later that year for the rebels. The government's response was at first confused, but culminated in the arming of the Arab militias that became known worldwide as the *janjawid.* International attempts to bring this war to an end are well documented: the string of drafts of United Nations Security Council Resolutions (some passed, fewer implemented); the protests; the accusations of genocide; the mediation efforts, failed ceasefires and peace agreements; and the deployment of troops with inadequate mandates and capabilities.[1]

Various attempts were made to broker ceasefires in talks in the Chadian capital, N'Djamena and eventually in Abuja, Nigeria. The Abuja talks continued for over a year, with no real engagement between the parties. One of many complications was the fact that the international 'friends' supporting the long-running talks in Kenya between the Khartoum regime and the southern rebel movement did not want the Darfur negotiations to distract from reaching an agreement between north and south. Yet when the Comprehensive Peace Agreement between north and south had been signed, the expectation of the Darfur armed groups was to reach a similar deal, even though the content of the CPA in effect did not allow this. Catch-22!

This was the stalled situation until the impatient mediators, backed by even more impatient third-party governments, insisted that the parties must meet the last of many deadlines that had been set for an agreement. The parties were presented with a text and five days to agree to sign it. After a forty-eight-hour extension of the deadline, the government and just one of the three rebel movements – perhaps the least significant of them – agreed to sign. The leader of this group was projected to instant fame, as he was rewarded with the supposedly fourth most powerful position in the Presidency, an official house in Khartoum, offices and cars, and a meeting at the White House with President George W. Bush. Meanwhile, the other armed movements vehemently rejected this Darfur Peace Agreement, and, while international diplomats tried to get them to sign it, the acronym DPA became a dirty word among the Darfurian opposition.

Outside the tent

And then there was Concordis International. This was a strange time for us as we worked to support the peace process 'from the outside'. Representatives of the armed movements were telling us, 'There wasn't really much of the content of the DPA that we objected to, it was the way it was forced on us. It wasn't *our* agreement.' When we went to governments and asked them to fund our attempts to bring the parties together informally, with no strings attached, they asked us, 'How will you draft the Annex to the DPA that you hope to get them to sign?' 'We weren't planning to mention the DPA,' I replied.

The story of the Darfurian engagement of Concordis International illustrates both the strength and the weakness of unofficial diplomacy. Back in 2003, on the foundation of Concordis' previous work over several years with Sudanese, many of whom included Darfurians, we were convinced by our Darfurian friends of the need for informal, unofficial dialogue between makers and influencers of policy from the region. These meetings would explore the conflict issues and act in support of official talks, if they ever got going. Such dialogue would also help to lay the groundwork for negotiations, and make them more likely to take place and be successful.

We tried unsuccessfully to interest governments and other major donors in funding such work. Eventually, with some frustration, we gave up on this and turned to the churches. At that time, mid-2004, Darfur was in the news and many churches were being asked to support feeding and housing the refugees and the internally displaced in camps. We argued, in letters to a number of churches, that such relief work was necessary and important, but was essentially closing the stable door after the horse was long gone. Our own work, although much less certain in terms of concrete outcomes, was aimed at preventing the conflict so that this suffering would not occur again in the first place. The argument struck a chord in many churches, even though our activity was far from what might be described as 'mission'. One large church in Bristol devoted the entire collection one Sunday to Concordis, and a tiny church in Norfolk with about fifteen members made a remarkably generous donation. I was delighted that the first of our Darfur-focused 'consultations', as we call them, was funded by the Christian church.

In this first meeting, we brought together Darfurians and other interested Sudanese to work on questions of land use and tenure, a relatively technical and non-controversial subject. They included men and women from the government of Sudan, from the armed resistance movements and from civil society, backed up by recognized experts in the field of semi-arid land use. Widely recognized today, but less so then, as one of the key issues underlying the conflict in Darfur, the competition over meagre land resources, against the background of decreasing and more variable rainfall, is part of a complex web of causes of conflict. The traditional means of dealing with this competition, particularly between settled farmers and pastoralists who migrated with their herds of camels or cattle, had been eroded by environmental pressures and other factors. The inroads of modernity had challenged traditional authority structures, for instance, by allowing and encouraging individual ownership of land, a resource in which the culture of each tribe is deeply rooted. Periods of drought in the 1970s and 1980s increased the pressure.

These were just some of the themes at this first consultation, which led to urgent requests for more of the same. We were able to raise funds for a further two Darfur consultations. The second focused on the political, cultural and economic marginalization of Darfur, which had been identified at the first meeting as another important cause of rightful grievance and conflict. For the third consultation, we had gained enough trust with our participants and felt we had built sufficient confidence between them to move closer to the more sensitive, security-related issues. We entitled this consultation 'Enabling the Sustainable and Safe Return and Reintegration of the Displaced in Darfur', and focused on the many obstacles to getting the several million displaced Darfurians back to their home villages and areas. Clearly, a sense of security was the key, but this was founded on solving a wide range of problems like police training, environmental management, rebuilding agriculture, the provision of water resources and improving the effectiveness of international troops, not to speak of the overarching political issues. Even the relatively good conditions provided by international agencies in the camps were seen as a reason for people not to return home.

Ironically, given the unknown coming failure of the Abuja talks, the overall tenor of the consultation was positive and hopeful. A Declaration of Principles had been agreed at Abuja, and our participants expressed their wish to move beyond blaming and shaming, beyond demonization and condemnation. They spoke of common values, mutual respect and Sudanese history. They thanked Concordis for having helped to bring peace to southern Sudan through its contribution to the process that led to the Comprehensive Peace Agreement, for its inclusive and in-depth studies of the issues underlying the conflict, and for encouraging the tone of reconciliation.

Participants spoke of Sudan's need to reconcile its ethnic and religious diversity and its consequent multiple visions for the future. They also emphasized that neither the rebel movements in Darfur nor the government, who were negotiating in Abuja over the political future of Darfur, represented all the people in Darfur. In contrast, our consultations included former governors of Darfur and of its three constituent states, representatives of rebel groups, former government ministers, leaders of women's organizations, academics and civil society leaders.

Getting to talking

We ended the last chapter with the idea that policy dialogue is one of several elements of comprehensive peace-building, and this is another name for the unofficial or 'track two' diplomacy which is the main focus of Concordis International. Given my personal links with the organization, I make no excuse for devoting this chapter to Concordis.

The rationale for what we do derives from two roots. The first is the choice of the influential middle level of leadership in a conflictual society as defined by John Paul Lederach, which I have already described in some detail. For the second we can thank Dr Michael Schluter, who founded a Christian think tank, the Jubilee Centre, in Cambridge over a quarter-century ago, and has developed what he calls relationism on the foundation of the relationships between Father, Son and Holy Spirit within the Trinity.[2]

Essentially, this is not complicated. Michael rightly emphasizes that, in public life, relationships are as important as the financial bottom line. A very specific application of this principle was put into practice by Michael and others in their work in the 1980s with South Africans, as a major contribution to the peaceful transition from apartheid to majority rule. Before there was any real contact between black and white South Africans, they brought influential individuals together outside the country to work together on banking, land reform and other obstacles to progress. Subsequently, the group worked for three years with Rwandans on issues of agriculture and post-conflict justice, to help bring both practical reconstruction and mental and spiritual healing following the horrific genocide in their country. Their reputation went before them to Sudan, where they were invited to start the similar work that eventually became Concordis International, and where we are working still, both nationally and for regions like Darfur.

Sudan is the main, but not the only, area of activity, and we remain open to potential situations where our approach can make a difference. We are currently building up a project with a Kenyan partner, focusing initially on issues of land ownership that were one of the factors in the post-election violence in 2008. However, we have often been unable to respond to requests for our help in other parts of the world.

The vision we have identified for ourselves is 'to work alongside those affected by armed conflict in the world, building consensus on the issues that divide and enabling them to create lasting peace and hope for their shared future'. Put in another way, the twin aims of the work we do are to achieve long-term transformation of relationships across conflict boundaries, through building relationships of trust between an inclusive group of influential individuals – Lederach's second-level leaders – and to help that group work together to find common ground on ways of dealing with the deep-rooted issues underlying the conflict.

To achieve this, we consciously use Michael Schluter's concepts of relational proximity. He writes of five elements that go towards building a constructive relationship, be it in the home, in business or in a war zone.

- First is **directness**, the commitment to quality of communication, to direct personal contact. E-mails, letters, phone calls and faxes have their place, but can not fully replace face-to-face contact.
- Second is **continuity**, investment in 'shared time over time', in the stability of the contacts over a protracted period.
- Michael rather grandly names the third element **multiplexity**, meaning that relationships thrive when contact takes place in a variety of social contexts, where a breadth of mutual knowledge and shared experience can be achieved between the parties.
- The fourth element involves the reduction of power differentials, so that mutual respect can be maintained, in other words, the maintenance of **parity** within the context of the encounter.
- Michael's final element is **commonality**, whereby a sense of common purpose is encouraged based on some level of shared identity, so that differences are respected.

These concepts are founded on solid research, and we have found at Concordis that if they are applied pragmatically as a whole, they do form a genuine basis for developing relationships.

Sticking to the values

This relational approach is not the whole basis of our work, of course. We have developed other principles and values, the most important of which are a non-partisan approach and long-term engagement.

Dealing with such controversial matters as the horrors of Darfur, I soon had to face the question of whether we as an organization should speak out against this or that perpetrator. I was helped, early in my time at Concordis, by watching a mediation organization get into a very public exchange of increasingly vitriolic press releases with an African government, which led to the collapse of the planned mediation. 'If you want to be trusted as non-partisan, better keep quiet,' I thought, and determined that we would not make press statements unless absolutely necessary, and that we would avoid public advocacy as an organization, whatever our personal views. I have never regretted this. There are plenty of organizations in the world making a noise about the injustices that are all around us, and I hope that their cries have some effect, but our tiny organizational voice would make little difference to the overall sound level.

The long-term approach was already important to Concordis' predecessor organization (Newick Park Initiative), and became even more so to me. It is possible for organizations to chase after a crisis situation and perhaps after the associated crisis funding. They can arrive in a conflict area without detailed understanding of the issues, perhaps do more harm than good, and leave again when the funding dries up. The Concordis approach is different. Where our contribution is welcomed and resources allow, we seek to commit ourselves to long-term engagement with the communities involved in a conflict situation. There is a price to be paid for this: we have to do what can be done with the limited funding available, and often in situations where our work is not meeting the immediate political goals of any major donor.

Some of our other values might be seen as making a virtue out of necessity. We recognize that we are small. We are unable to have a major direct effect at the grassroots level of a society – in the villages and communities – so we focus our limited resources at the policy level where they can have most impact, developing relationships between senior individuals who are influential in their respective constituencies. At this level, shared knowledge is important, so we aim to build consensus on the basis of top-quality, in-depth research, undertaken where possible by members of the communities involved in the conflict, but supplemented by international expertise. However, if the overall impact is to become a reality, it is also important that our work at the middle level has strong links to the political leadership and to the grassroots. So we need to connect with community-level organizations, cooperate and try to achieve synergy.

Our size also means that we need to make best use of limited resources, so we keep the core organization small and flexible, and supplement it by out-sourcing arrangements, project staff, consultants, volunteers and interns. For the same reason, we avoid wasting energy and actively seek collaboration with other organizations undertaking similar or connected work, and try thereby to achieve synergy of effort. 'You people,' said an American expert in conflict resolution to me one day at a conference, 'make money go further than almost anyone else I know.' That made me feel better about some of our scrimping and saving.

The kernel of our work is a series of low-profile consultations, on neutral ground and lasting perhaps several days, where participants are invited to engage with one another on one or more conflict issues. The 'residential' aspect of the consultations is important, allowing participants to engage with one another in a range of different contexts and not just at the conference table. They attend in their personal capacities: in other words, they do not have to state the party line of their organization or government, but can share ideas freely with their opponents. We make sure that expertise is available on the issues, if necessary from outside. Typically, the group will number up to about thirty key 'mid-level' participants. Above that number, the group dynamics become much more difficult. To bring together an inclusive group of this size, representative of the society in conflict, can be a real challenge. Often, the problem is not finding participants but deciding whom to exclude, as news of the meeting spreads. We try to keep the news off the mobile phone networks for as long as possible.

What is success?

Requirements from potential donors to demonstrate concrete outcomes from our work are very difficult to satisfy. Evidence is often anecdotal. At the consultation that started off our other Sudanese regional work, with the eastern Sudanese from the other side of the country, a senior Sudanese opposition leader told me this was the first time in twelve years he had shaken the hand of someone from the Khartoum regime. And at the same consultation I was told that a senior group was meeting quietly in one another's homes in Khartoum as a result of our early work on Darfur.

How do you measure success? One of our 'success stories', where we provided a service that met the political requirements of a group of governments, was this work with the eastern Sudanese. We had been trying for some months to get a hearing for our view that the rumbling civil war in the east had at least the potential to escalate, if not to become the 'next Darfur'. Eventually, we gained funding for a consultation that brought together eastern Sudanese from government, armed rebels and political opposition. It was a small group, but the participants agreed a development framework that could form the potential basis of a peace agreement, since one of the few grievances the rebels could agree among themselves related to economic marginalization and poverty.

As a result, we were asked to bring the government and the main remaining rebel group together for informal negotiations. Months of jockeying for position and quibbling about the format of the talks followed, until Concordis was asked to provide workshops for the divided rebels to help them become more unified, more constructive and better prepared for potential negotiations to be mediated by someone else. We fulfilled our mission, in three weeks of sometimes harrowing, sometimes bizarrely anarchic experience in the Eritrean capital, Asmara. Thanks in part to our preparation, the rebels agreed to sit down and negotiate with the government, did so under Eritrean mediation and signed the Eastern Sudan Peace Agreement in October 2006. A successful pre-negotiation contribution by Concordis! Yet we were unable to control the agreement that was signed, or even to contribute directly to its content, and the 'quality' of the agreement left a lot to be desired. Arguably, the main factor that made the agreement possible was the change of Eritrean policy from supporting the eastern Sudanese rebels to encouraging them to make a deal. Yet our role in getting a process started and nursing it on its way was a key piece of the jigsaw. We would have liked to have run a follow-up consultation on the implementation of the agreement to relieve poverty in eastern Sudan, but funding was not available.

Today, we continue to work on Sudan, doing what we can to support the implementation of the 2005 agreement, as the end of the six-year transition period draws frighteningly close without the progress towards sustained peace that had been hoped for. Analysts and pundits comment on the lack of progress, and make doom-laden prognoses for the next few years. They may be right, but it is easy to analyse and comment, to identify the problems, to lay blame for the failures. There is a place for people who are working with a more positive, constructive approach, bringing in the element of hope, looking for the 'best-case scenario', as one of the pioneers of 'track two diplomacy' once put it. This is the Concordis approach.

Weak and strong

The Concordis approach has advantages and disadvantages, both of which are related to our position of relative weakness, which brings us back to the questions of power that we explored earlier. One of our Sudanese (Muslim) friends once likened Concordis to David against Goliath, an image that has stuck in my mind for several years. Apart from our experience of chronic underfunding in our first five years, it is also true that we are not in a position to apply pressure or incentives to conflict parties. But our very weakness can enhance our reputation for impartiality and can build trust.

Sometimes, our reputation with those involved in the conflict has been more positive than with external officials and diplomats who have been tasked with 'sorting out' the problem. Our work is intended to support official negotiations in two main ways. Firstly, it provides a bedrock of solid knowledge and 'owned' consensus on some of the issues that contribute to causing conflict but which are often difficult to translate into negotiating positions. Secondly and more importantly, by bringing together the broader society, which is often not represented at the negotiating table, we help to provide the link between the restricted number of groups – often those who have taken up arms – who sit at the table with the wider society they purport to represent. In a sense, we help to give a voice to those who have not taken up arms.

This is not always appreciated by officials. Perhaps they see such 'help' as an unnecessary distraction from their main goal: getting an agreement. Perhaps they are concerned about the conflict parties 'shopping around' for the most attractive option. Whatever the reason, the acceptance by officials of our work, however well thought of it is by those involved in the conflict, has fluctuated from grudging recognition through scepticism to outright hostility. Raising funds in this environment, for what is a relatively low-cost endeavour but with uncertain outcomes, makes one think of blood and stones.

Biblical basis

Concordis is not constitutionally a Christian organization and many of those who have worked in it would not profess any faith, but it has a strong Christian heritage. This is one of the reasons why I think it important for us to maintain our links with the organizations from which we sprang, the Jubilee Centre and the Relationships Foundation.[3] Our approach is also derived from biblical principles and many of the individuals, churches, community groups and trusts who generously support us do so out of their Christian commitment to peacemaking.

So from where does this Christian foundation derive? There are several strands. First is of course the relational approach described above, derived from the knowledge that our God is a relational God. As important are the values that underpin our work: values such as equality, justice, mercy and reconciliation, which we learn from the Bible. Also, we do our best to approach our work with some concept of service and, I hope, humility, not at all claiming to have the answers to the problems that have caused pain and division to a society, but rather being available to help both those who have suffered and those who have caused the suffering to work together constructively. We take a long-term approach to developing peace, recognizing that it is much more than just the cessation of violence; to bring violence to an end there needs to be movement towards wholeness, towards *šālôm*. And finally the recognition that power and strength are not everything, that there is a place for weakness, has a biblical root.

I have often tentatively thought to observe God's hand in our circumstances, although that is the kind of claim about which I am naturally very cautious. The effort and investment we put into research and networking in preparation for a potential Afghanistan project, for example, appeared at the time to be wasted. Recent developments from an unexpected direction, though, have allowed us to contribute to peacemaking in Afghanistan and to make use of some of that knowledge.

Peace-building sometimes seems to be a never-ending process. It would be convenient to think that we could simply find what was causing the problems, work out the solutions and implement them. Problem solved!

Peace-building sometimes seems to be a never-ending process. It would be convenient to think that we could simply find what was causing the problems, work out the solutions and implement them. Problem solved!

It is tempting for me as a trained engineer to think in these terms. Perhaps some of the churches that contributed to our early Darfur work wonder if their money was well spent, because we haven't 'solved' the Darfur problem. Yet humanity is not like that. Dealing with conflict is more like a continuous battle, with some forces working against peace, and the need for us and others to be constantly working on the side of peace. This is why, as I have said elsewhere, I find it difficult to see how anyone can do this kind of work for any length of time without some concept of God's sovereignty and providence. This is especially true for the long-term perspectives needed to work towards reconciliation, the subject of our next chapter.

8 BE RECONCILED

'All this is from God, who reconciled us to himself through Christ and gave us the ministry of reconciliation.' 2 Corinthians 5:18

'Reconciliation is a process, it's not an event. It's something that's going to be happening over decades.' Archbishop Desmond Tutu, interviewed on 'Sunday' Programme, BBC Radio 4, 31 May 2009

Musalaha

Those who visit Dr Salim Munayer in his office in Jerusalem encounter an atmosphere of energetic activity, with young volunteers working at computer screens, under brightly coloured pictures of Israeli and Palestinian teenagers trekking or riding camels together through a desert landscape. Someone will find time to show you a video of the work of Musalaha (Arabic for reconciliation) or to explain a little of what the organization does.

Musalaha is a non-profit-making organization led by Dr Munayer, which the website describes as seeking 'to promote reconciliation between Israelis and Palestinians as demonstrated in the life and teaching of Jesus'. Musalaha seeks 'to be an encouragement and facilitator of reconciliation, first among Palestinian Christians and Messianic Israelis, and then beyond to our respective communities'.[1] Now, to imagine that this is not political would be a mistake. Although there

is a strong tradition of Christianity among the Palestinian
people, the Christians are by no means seen as in the fore-
front of the struggle for Palestinian freedom and dignity.
On the Israeli side, mention of Jews who have accepted the
claims of Jesus as Messiah generally brings either a hostile
response or a look of studied puzzlement. However, these
two groups have something in common that provides a
bridge across the divide.

The work of Musalaha is a corrective to the divisions
between Christians in the Holy Land. Christians from outside
who visit Israel tend to come down on one side or the other,
sometimes unwittingly, influenced either by the theology
of Christian Zionism or by a sympathy for the plight of
Palestinians. Even the Church of England divides along
these lines. Among the many churches of different denominations in Jerusalem, Christchurch near the Jaffa Gate and St
George's Cathedral outside the Damascus Gate represent the
two ends of the Anglican spectrum here. I have stayed in the
guest house of each of them and felt an affinity with both, as
I grappled with the competing viewpoints.

For almost twenty years, Musalaha has been providing
space for encounters and training in reconciliation. Starting
by taking groups of Palestinians and Israelis into isolated
locations in the desert and 'forcing' them to work together
away from their normal environment, Musalaha has developed a range of activities designed to build relationships
of trust. With a major focus on youth and young adults,
Musalaha today runs desert encounters, training workshops
and conferences, helping participants to recognize the basic
humanity of the 'other'. The organization also coordinates
Israeli–Palestinian women's networks, facilitating seminars and conferences for reconciliation training, and runs
summer camps that allow Israeli and Palestinian children

to meet, perhaps for the first time, in a safe environment. Although the primary focus has been on Christian believers from both sides of the divide, Salim Munayer explained to me how Musalaha's reputation has spread. Leaders of the broader communities have expressed an interest in learning about reconciliation, a step on the way to fulfilling Munayer's dream of achieving reconciliation between Israelis and Palestinians through the action of the Christian believers among them.

Making reconciliation happen

The final major theme of this book, reconciliation, is in many ways the most challenging and also the one where our Christian faith has most to say. The desire for reconciliation does not belong only to Christians, and there has been an increased interest among conflict resolution specialists and academics in this most difficult and, to many, nebulous subject. Nonetheless, the forgiveness and restoration of relationships that lie at the heart of reconciliation are central to the Christian faith.

Why nebulous? One way to answer this question is to imagine the various different means of engaging with armed conflict as a spectrum. Hizkias Assefa of Eastern Mennonite University does this. At one end of his spectrum is the use of military force to suppress the conflict, to put a lid on it, and the spectrum then develops through adjudication, arbitration, negotiation and mediation, finishing up at the other extreme with reconciliation.[2] Now, I suspect that his choice of activities here and the way he constructs the spectrum are much too simple, but the overall principle is true enough. Assefa identifies three aspects that change as we move along this spectrum. First, the degree of involvement of the conflict participants in the process is at its least at the 'suppression' end of the spectrum – of course – and at a maximum at the reconciliation end. Secondly, the durability of the solutions reached increases as you move along the spectrum from enforced conflict suppression to reconciliation, something we would instinctively expect to be the case. But thirdly, says Assefa, as we move along that spectrum, our knowledge and understanding of the approaches to be used becomes 'sketchy, less developed and unsystematic'.

So we have something in reconciliation that the conflict resolution and peace-building experts increasingly see as important, that they often admit to understanding very imperfectly, and where they see much of the expertise lying with the 'religious' communities. I am not so sure about 'religion', but let's see how our Christian faith, recognizing the evil in the world but confident in the hope of better things, can contribute something here. Because, although many of those who do their best to deal with violent conflict see reconciliation as essential to establishing long-term peace and stability, they also see it as nigh-on impossible to achieve. And many see those who attempt to achieve reconciliation as naïve optimists.

The aim of this chapter, then, is to survey this field quite comprehensively: to see what conflict management research, experience of practice and prayerful engagement can bring to our understanding. After trying to establish some shared understanding of what reconciliation actually is, we will look back to the relevance of the 'new wars' of the post-Cold War era to the subject, then consider what conflict theorists have to say, particularly those who specialize in transitional justice. Finally, apology and forgiveness deserve a section all of their own.

We will certainly try to survey what our Christian faith has to say specifically on reconciliation, looking at a few examples where these concepts have been put into practice, as we try to connect up the dots and attempt the perhaps impossible task of working out how we can approach reconciliation as a whole. Just to set the scene, though, let's put reconciliation in perspective through what is one of the key Bible verses relating to this subject, which captures some of the essence: Psalm 85:10, where we read that 'Mercy and truth have met together; righteousness and peace have kissed'.[3] These four elements of reconciliation – mercy, truth, righteousness (or justice) and peace – seem to be like four intertwined strands of a rope, or four tributaries of a river flowing together and intermingling at the confluence, as their apparent opposition to each other is overcome by their common purpose.

What does reconciliation mean?

So what is reconciliation? There are a number of definitions, coming from Christian and other sources.

It is perhaps no surprise that reconciliation is seen by secular experts as on the one hand essential, but on the other difficult or impossible, because, as Robert Schreiter says, reconciliation has two faces, a social one that has to do with 'providing structures and processes whereby a fractured society can be reconstructed as truthful and just', and a spiritual one 'that has to do with rebuilding shattered lives *so that* social reconciliation becomes a reality'.[4] A tall order!

We will focus first and foremost on the social aspect, but recognize, as does Schreiter, that the spiritual face is essential to the social one. As for a definition, I suspect that John Paul Lederach's will serve as well as any, because it captures both the social and the spiritual (or at least individual) element, it emphasizes the relational aspects and it recognizes that reconciliation is a process and not a finished state of affairs. And it is mercifully short. Lederach defines reconciliation as the 'dynamic, adaptive process of rebuilding interpersonal and community relationships'.

One could argue that all reconciliation is about individuals, that reconciliation is achieved one person at a time, and I would not disagree with that, but there is also value in thinking about reconciliation in damaged *societies*, especially in a book about Christian approaches to armed conflict.

Later we will look at the elements of reconciliation. First, though, let's consider the modern context for all of this: post-Cold War conflict.

'New wars' and reconciliation

Mary Kaldor's description of 'new wars' is again helpful here. At the outset we established that we were predominantly considering wars within, rather than between, states, and looked at the parallel effects of globalization and fragmentation. However, Kaldor took this further and showed how these 'new wars' have increasingly involved a range of non-state actors as well as state authorities, fighting over issues of ideology, resources and identity. As a result, the conflict is characterized by the deliberate targeting of civilians, through genocide, rape, ethnic cleansing and displacement, to mobilize group identity and to demonize and dehumanize other groups. And because of international crime, refugee pressures, human trafficking and drug smuggling, these are instabilities we are unable to ignore, even if we are not directly involved.

How does this affect the need for reconciliation?

Because the fighting groups are not divided by national borders, but in close contact with each other, sharing the same territory, they cannot simply be separated. In many cases they may have lived together as neighbours for decades before being driven apart, often through political manipulation of

what were, viewed objectively, relatively insignificant differences. So if the differences were so small and the prior
relationships comparatively positive, there would appear to
be good grounds for optimism that reconciliation might be
successful. Yet the often horrific nature of the actions that
have been perpetrated means that a wedge of animosity has
been driven between these communities.

As we've seen, a ceasefire or a political settlement, even if
backed up by a peacekeeping force, is never enough. There
must be work to deal with the underlying causes of the conflict, policy changes to put right the inequities, the unfairness
that may have led, however indirectly, to the conflict. But
this is not enough either. The longer the violence continues,
the more extreme it seems to become. Setting aside all of
the effects that tend to prolong and deepen violence – the
brutalization, the displacement from normal livelihoods,
the conflict entrepreneurship – there is still a sense in which
the accumulation of horrors develops an ever-increasing
resentment and hatred. So this type of war, where the civilian suffering is an integral part of the war-fighting, leads to an
increased need for reconciliation and an increased difficulty
in achieving it.

It is worth reminding ourselves, however, that this is not
a simple sequence: ceasefire, political settlement, reconstruction, righting inequalities and unfairness, then reconciliation.
In a sense, we may sometimes have to stand the sequence
on its head. Without reconciliation, none of the other steps
may be possible. For example, the relatively successful
Oslo process led to the Oslo Accords, a historic agreement
between the political leaders, Yitzak Rabin and Yassir Arafat.
Yet peace rapidly gave way to suicide bombings and reprisals.
Many have criticized the content of the agreement, but one
of the key reasons for the failure of the Oslo Accords to bring

peace between Israelis and Palestinians was the continuing animosity between the two societies.[5] We could assert this even more strongly for the later Geneva Accord, which informally identified the elements of a comprehensive final-status agreement, but more or less sank without trace because it lacked political support.

Yet we have reason to believe that God is capable of overcoming these barriers, and one of the ways he does so is through the various elements of reconciliation.

Reconciliation in all its parts

Focusing on the post-conflict scenario, Professor Andrew Rigby of Coventry University describes the three ingredients needed for a process of post-conflict social reconciliation to be successful.

- First, there needs to be a sense of peace and security, leaving violence behind as a means of solving differences.
- An element of truth-telling is needed, which involves the acknowledgment of past wrongs and, to some extent, construction of a shared understanding of history.
- Finally, there must be *some* recognition that justice has been done, through punishment or reparation or both.

Andrew Rigby's academic research is in no way taking a Christian viewpoint here and is focusing very much on the social issues. So, although his insight is extremely valuable, the essential spiritual aspect is missing. I may be doing Andrew a disservice, because if you saw his work in more detail I think you would find that he definitely recognizes the need for individual healing of pain. Also of note here is the fact that his description of the ingredients is very broad and

non-prescriptive, and leaves a great deal open for interpretation and cultural adjustment. This is very wise, because a
great deal of trouble has been caused in the past by imposition of Western paradigms of justice on to societies that are
already well served by their own concepts. Just as the best
of Western missionaries nowadays are able to disentangle
their Western cultural baggage from the actual gospel, so we
should be able to avoid a kind of judicial imperialism.

These three elements, stability, truth and justice, may
seem to be in chronological sequence, and in a sense they are,
but it seems to me that all three elements need to be present
simultaneously. Yet they conflict with each other: another
conundrum. I am not sure there are easy answers here, but
Christians ought at least to be able to avoid being blink-
ered by our Western cultural outlook, and by the modern
emphasis on rights-based and litigious approaches to societal
issues. Not least because of the weakening of state sovereignty through 'Responsibility to Protect', the international
consensus on how a post-conflict state should deal with past
misdeeds now has a very powerful influence. We need to be
sure that the influence is not counter-productive.

What went before
Andrew Rigby's area of study is known as post-conflict justice
and reconciliation or as transitional justice, so it definitely
focuses on the situation after violent conflict. It was one of
the areas in which my predecessors at Concordis, then known
as the Newick Park Initiative, helped the Rwandans decide
on policies for dealing with over 120,000 accused individuals
following the 1994 genocide. Rwanda decided against a Truth
and Reconciliation Commission, and opted instead for the
local community courts known as *gacaca*. Here the accused
and their accusers are heard 'under a tree'. It is a fascinating

amalgam of truth-telling and prosecution aiming to achieve
some degree of reconciliation, as the local courts involve the
whole community in constructing an agreed narrative of
what took place, which can be a way of restoring community
relationships. The court can sentence the accused to prison
for up to thirty years, but acknowledgment of guilt can lead
to a decreased sentence, possibly taking the form of some
kind of community service. The outcomes are not perfect,
but the system has many strengths.

Without going into greater detail in a very complex area,
this one example shows the contrast between different forms
of justice: between criminal justice, restorative justice and
even social/economic justice; and between local traditional
and international modern justice. In a very simplistic way,
we can see the potential negative impact of the work of international courts on the possibility of reconciliation in complex
civil wars. The involvement of the International Criminal
Court in Northern Uganda is a case in point.

The most famous example of dealing with the past is
the South African Truth and Reconciliation Commission.
Arguably, its very fame has had an ambivalent international
impact. Partly because of Desmond Tutu's charisma and the
amount of publicity it has received, it has contributed to the
popular international belief that such a commission, based
on the South African model, is the only way to deal with
the past. In fact, there have been many Truth Commissions
around the world with different emphases – Chile and
Morocco to name but two – and many other ways of dealing
with the past.

There are strong opinions and no clear agreement on
whether it is better for a society to forget the past or to face
it. Both have been tried – in Mozambique and South Africa,
for example – and both have their strengths and weaknesses.

It is difficult to argue conclusively that the two countries that have in effect opted for a form of official amnesia, post-civil war Mozambique and post-Franco Spain, have suffered through their choice. Cambodia is a similar but more complex case. Nonetheless, there are signs that the Spanish past, for example, has not simply gone away, and that the amnesia, even if it was officially sanctioned, has been only temporary.

Perhaps the answer is different for each post-conflict state, where atrocities have been committed in the heat of war. That was the premise of a consultation we at Concordis International ran in 2007 for an inclusive group of influential Sudanese participants, of all political and religious persuasions, in the tranquil environment of Ammerdown in Somerset. Our aim was to provide space for these Sudanese men and women to work together towards genuinely Sudanese answers to the questions that had been answered with the Truth and Reconciliation Commission in South Africa but differently elsewhere.[6]

Several of the participants were from the Darfur region. All recognized – and we are well aware through our continuing work with the ongoing conflict there – that it is not currently appropriate in Darfur to be speaking of 'post-conflict' anything. Nationally, though, there is a peace agreement and it can never be too early for a society faced with such issues to start thinking about questions of impunity and accountability, justice and mercy, retribution and forgiveness. This was certainly the view of our participants at Ammerdown, who saw the consultation as just the first step in a process of dialogue on these issues. We have been asked, for example, to help the Sudan Inter-religious Council in dialogue and training on the role of religious leaders in encouraging reconciliation.

There is much more to be said on the subject of

post-conflict justice than I have room for here, but I have quite deliberately devoted some space to this aspect of social reconciliation. It would be a mistake to imagine that we can speak about Christian reconciliation as if it were in some way a separate issue, unconnected with questions of justice, amnesty, impunity and political power. Nevertheless, there is a distinctive Christian view of reconciliation, and at its heart stands forgiveness.

To forgive is divine

Let me start by emphasizing the direct link between our for-giving others and God forgiving us. We read in the Gospel of Matthew: 'But if you do not forgive men their sins, your Father will not forgive your sins.'[7] It looks rather like a threat, but it is actually more a statement of fact. We will not delve into the theology in any detail, but I think this is actually saying that we cannot find – or even ask – forgiveness from God without the repentance that automatically goes with our own forgiving attitude. So we can not expect God to forgive us until we have done our own forgiving.

There are essentially three ways we can deal with anger. We can take revenge on the perpetrator, we can make the conscious decision to forgive, or we can sit on our anger for hours, days, years or even decades. The third option may of course be simply delaying one of the other two, probably at some cost to our own emotional stability, as bitterness deepens and festers. Making one of these three choices is no doubt part of personal experience for every one of us on an almost daily basis. We all know we should forgive, but somehow it is never that easy.

There are many societies where forgiveness is a sign of weakness, and vengeance is seen as a necessary part of indi-vidual, family or clan honour. In any traumatized society where loved ones have been killed, to forgive may be seen as betrayal of the dead. In a sense, we do not have the right to forgive on behalf of those to whom the wrong was done. This is the central theme of Simon Wiesenthal's book *The Sunflower*, where he finds himself unable to forgive a dying and genuinely repentant Nazi soldier for the atrocities he committed in the Holocaust. Ultimately, only God has that right. We do, though, have the right and responsibility to forgive wrongs done to us personally, so relatives can, for example, forgive the pain caused to them by the loss. But this is a very difficult thing to do, and a personal matter, so none of us has the right to tell others to forgive, and indeed there is not much point in doing so.

The capability to forgive is a grace given to us by God. In extreme situations, which I hope and pray that few of us will ever have to experience, this grace may be given gradually as part of a progressive process of healing. It may take us a long time to get to this point, and perhaps a first step in the process is to ask God to forgive the wrong, following the example of Jesus himself as he was being crucified, and of the first Christian martyr, Stephen, when he was being stoned. Forgiveness is not at all the same thing as condoning, excusing or minimizing the offence. Indeed, at the core of forgiveness is a recognition of the truth of what has been done, not 'forgiving and forgetting', but rather a transformation of the genuine memory of the event.

The capability to forgive is a grace given to us by God.

Apology and forgiveness

What if the transgressor does not admit that he or she has wronged the victim? Is apology necessary for forgiveness? In theory, it is not. Many of us will remember the challenging example set by Gordon Wilson, who quietly but publicly showed that he bore no grudge against the IRA killers of his daughter at Enniskillen, and did not demand an apology. But if we ourselves are the perpetrators, we should remember that apology – acknowledgment of wrongdoing – makes forgiveness easier and is a very powerful step on the road to reconciliation.[8]

Apology may be too easy an option, if not accompanied by restitution, but the opposite may also be true. When in 1997 the Australian government set aside a $40m package of measures to recompense Aboriginals for racist abuse of the 'stolen generation' of children removed from their birth mothers, the move was criticized despite the substantial compensation, because of the government's failure to apologize. Some ten years later, Prime Minister Kevin Rudd did apologize, and the gesture was seen as very significant.

Apology is just a symbolic act, but symbolism can be very powerful. Through making apologies, people and organizations hope to achieve one or more purposes. Particularly at the individual level, the aim can simply be to obtain forgiveness for wrongs done, because guilt can fester, or to achieve closure in a dispute. Other motives can be more circumspect: to restore national reputation or a business's corporate image, to defuse a volatile situation or to forestall retribution. Seen more positively as a constructive future-oriented act, an apology can also have the aim of establishing accountability and encouraging a positive future relationship. So apology can be a starting point for healing, even if reconciliation is not yet possible.

There are of course those who argue against the whole trend towards public historical apology. They suggest that it is divisive to stir up past hatreds, and that people who did not commit the wrongs themselves should not apologize for atrocities committed by their forebears. However, there has been an increasing recognition that taking responsibility for wrongs committed in the past does actually matter. Many apologies are official, made on behalf of a nation or a corporation, but some are undertaken by groups of individuals. One striking example is the Reconciliation Walk, a three-year trek by different Christian groups along the route of the first Crusade. On reaching Jerusalem, the walk culminated in a ceremony of apology for the Crusades to Jews, Orthodox Christians and Muslims, marking the 900th anniversary of the First Crusade in 1999. This regret, honestly expressed, for 'atrocities committed in the name of Christ by our predecessors' was clearly focused on future healing of relationships and has led to a number of other reconciliation activities.

So apology has power. It symbolically encourages thinking constructively about the past and makes the historical narrative more complete. The power can be diminished, though, when apology is given only in response to repeated demands for it, or when the way it is expressed is incomplete, qualified, nuanced or defensive. And of course the absence of apology, when it is requested or expected, can further inflame the situation.

This brings us back to the question of forgiveness, because it is inevitably more difficult to forgive when the acknowledgment of the wrong is absent or given only grudgingly. We see this in the imperfect example of the South African Truth and Reconciliation Commission, particularly in the cases examined in the film *Long Night's Journey into Day*, where the mixture of motives of those acknowledging their crimes was very clear. Some were obviously only doing so in order to gain the promised amnesty, with no signs of genuine remorse or repentance. The truth about the past was exposed, and relatives of victims could find out what had happened to their loved ones, but reconciliation was at best incomplete. In some cases, one gained the impression that the Commission's effect was to punish the victims a second time.

To return to the question posed above, is it possible to forgive without the perpetrator acknowledging the wrong? The answer must be that it is indeed possible, even if difficult, and as Christians we should follow God's example of unconditional forgiveness in this. If forgiveness occurs without repentance, there is in effect no reconciliation, so where does forgiveness fit in the whole reconciliation process? Ideally, repentance should lead to apology, allowing forgiveness. But if it is possible for us to forgive unconditionally, this can be an alternative first step in the reconciliation process, because the power of unwarranted forgiveness can prompt remorse, repentance and ultimately reconciliation.

Much of this is expressed at the personal level, but this positioning of forgiveness in the reconciliation process is one of the links to the society level. As well as a specific decision, forgiveness is also part of the process that can free us from being ruled by the past. One of the keys here, as suggested by Robert Schreiter, is the presence in societal leadership of reconciled individuals who can picture such a future.[9]

In one sense, the whole question of forgiveness for us as individuals is not a problem. If we find ourselves in a position where forgiveness of major trauma or wrongdoing is needed, we will know what we have to do. Whether we have the courage and grace to do so is a different matter. But the question with respect to social reconciliation is more: what can be done by outsiders to help a reconciliation process take place? This is where Christians can offer some insights relevant to social reconciliation.

Christian approaches to reconciliation

It is not clear that the church has all of the answers to reconciliation – indeed, as we have seen, it has occasionally caused some of the problems. However, the right place to start is with our own reconciliation to God. We read in one of Paul's letters to Corinth: 'Therefore, if anyone is in Christ, he is a new creation; the old has gone, the new has come! All this is from God, who reconciled us to himself through Christ and gave us the ministry of reconciliation.'[10]

What is this ministry of reconciliation? I am not sure that it just means evangelism. We can be talking about reconciliation in many senses: our reconciliation with God; our reconciliation with ourselves and with our neighbour; the reconciliation of the creation; the reconciliation between communities and nations. And none of these will be complete until Christ comes again.

But in the context of this book, there is much we can learn from some valuable Christian experience of a ministry of reconciliation. Mark Leakey, who heads the Armed Forces Christian Union, has, like Salim Munayer, given this much thought. He and others have applied it through the work of the organization Flame International. The focus of Flame International's ministry is to work for healing, forgiveness and reconciliation, with local Christians who share the group's vision to see people healed from the pain and trauma caused by war. Through seminars and workshops, they seek to communicate the hope, forgiveness and reconciliation offered by Jesus Christ. The real kernel of Flame's ministry is prayer, and this helps to remind us not only that it is God who reconciles us to himself, but also that reconciliation between humans – for individuals and for all levels of society – comes from God.

This comes home very clearly in the book by Robert

Schreiter, who relates God's ministry of reconciliation to a Christian way of dealing with suffering. Reconciliation is best achieved by 'bringing our own story of suffering into contact with the story of the suffering, death and resurrection of Jesus Christ'. In particular, Schreiter illustrates this through the resurrection appearances of Jesus, a captivating idea from which I will try briefly to pick out one or two elements.

In the well-known story of the Road to Emmaus, Jesus accompanies two despondent ex-disciples who have given up all hope as a result of his execution.[11] 'We had hoped that he was the one to redeem Israel,' they say. He listens to them as they tell their story of pain and lost hope, and as they admit their confusion about the stories told by the women who had gone to the tomb. As they walk, Jesus progressively explains to them how the suffering Christ fits in to the history of Israel. They are starting to feel encouraged, 'their hearts burning within them', but they still do not know who the stranger is. They ask him to have supper with them, and only when he breaks the bread and serves them do they suddenly recognize him.[12]

So along the road, Jesus creates a space where they can tell their painful story, and then helps them to see the story in a different light, within the larger context. He enables them to transform their story. In their invitation to him to eat with them, there are hints of their restored humanity. And in the moment of breaking bread there is a moment of grace, transformation and sudden recognition.

Another resurrection appearance is the moment when Jesus appears on the shore of Lake Galilee and cooks breakfast for the disciples.[13] Here the disciples have gone back to their old lives in Galilee and seem to have given up any idea of continuing the ministry as 'fishers of men'. They seem at a loss, aimless, and they decide to go fishing. All night they try to catch fish. They seem to be trying to get over their pain and disappointment by returning to their old routine, but without success. Come morning, an apparent stranger calls to them from the shore, helps them to find fish, and cooks a lakeside breakfast for them. Here Jesus is providing hospitality, and he does not rush to the next step, where he questions Peter three times as to whether he loves him, and then tells him three times to 'feed my lambs'. Schreiter suggests that Jesus is in this way reconnecting Peter with himself and the community, and commissioning him to take his place again in the ministry. The threefold nature, connected to Peter's threefold denial, shows us the significance of ritual and symbolism in reconciliation.

These are not the only examples of resurrection appearances, but Schreiter uses them to suggest four steps in a process of reconciliation.

Elements of a ministry of reconciliation
Accompaniment
Hospitality
Reconnecting
Commissioning

The first two, accompaniment and hospitality, are steps in which outsiders can play a role in a ministry of reconciliation. By travelling, literally or metaphorically, with the victims, hearing their stories and gently helping them to find the meaning in their pain and suffering, the outsider helps the victims not to forget the past but in some way to transfigure it. However, even though there may be a moment of transformation, the process of recovering from the pain is going to be slow; and for this, the victim needs to be received in genuine hospitality. Here a welcoming community can provide a sense of safety, a means of dealing with memory and an assurance of hope. We can think of places like Corrymeela in Northern Ireland or Ammerdown near Bath.

The third and fourth elements of the ministry are undertaken by God rather than by human effort. Reconnecting the individual to humanity is often sudden and unexpected, like the recognition of the disciples at Emmaus, as they connect their stories to the 'big picture'. Finally, the commissioning for the future, taking the individual beyond passive victimhood, could in some surprising way be connected with the trauma, such as when the reconciled takes up reconciliation work.

I have deliberately used the ideas of Robert Schreiter to end this chapter, as I think them a genuine and helpful attempt to get beyond generalizations and platitudes, to identify some of the spiritual aspects of a reconciliation ministry. As we move on to draw together the threads of the many practical aspects of Christian engagement with conflict, it will be helpful to keep in mind the strand running through this chapter: the importance of prayer.

9 EFFECTIVE CHRISTIAN ENGAGEMENT IN TWENTY-FIRST-CENTURY CONFLICT

'Peace I leave with you; my peace I give you.' John 14:27

'Do not be daunted by the enormity of the world's grief. Do justly now. Love mercy now. You are not obligated to complete the work. Neither are you free to abandon it.' Instruction from the Talmud

When I hear people protesting about horrific atrocities, or see demonstrations about human rights, I generally sympathize with the cause, but I also find myself in sympathy with the diplomats and others who are already working on the issue. 'Yes,' I find myself silently asking the protesters, 'but what should they actually *do*?'

When I hear Christians and others state that the use of military force is wrong and at the same time I see the violence, injustices and outright evil in the world, I find myself asking, 'Yes, but what should we actually *do*?'

When I hear people talking about reconciliation or saying that everyone should aim to achieve it, the question that always springs to my mind is, 'Yes, but what do you actually *do*?'

Active peacemaking
In a sense, the main purpose of this book has been to explore some answers to these questions. Perhaps it is my engineering training, my military background or what I have seen in

six years of trying to 'do' peacemaking, but I get frustrated by those who are ready to say what is being done badly, but are less vocal about what should be done about it, and even less willing to get involved constructively themselves. Perhaps I am being unfair. I harbour some doubts about who really benefits from protest and demonstrations, and I admit to becoming impatient with endless analysis. On the other hand, it will be clear from what has gone before that I do not imagine that neat 'engineering' solutions are available to us in these complex issues. So we do need the analysis too. Action without proper understanding is likely to do more harm than good.

As well as drawing together the strands of the earlier chapters to look at making peacemaking effective, let's identify how we, as individuals and as groups of Christians bound together in churches, can work at the interconnections of peace, justice, truth and mercy to contribute to stability in the world. It is reconciliation that stands at the centre of this nexus.

Approaching reconciliation

In different ways, the whole of this book is focused on aspects of the approach to reconciliation. We've just looked at the issue of reconciliation through a number of lenses, trying to find some answers to the question, 'What do you actually do?' However, here I will try to give a broader perspective on the issue. How is this reconciliation linked to Just War, pacifism, military intervention, non-military intervention and relational peace-building?

We set the scene by looking at the types of warfare that are most prevalent in the twenty-first century. Modern communications and media will not allow us to ignore these 'new wars', with their impact on the poor and helpless. We are challenged by the need to take some action. Yet what can we do?

First of all, we have to clarify in our own minds what we believe to be the moral basis on which we are free to act, or support others in their action. Should we, for example, decide that all violence, all armed force, is against the laws of God? I did not come to this conclusion, even though those who reach this decision deserve my respect. The model that I find most helpful in establishing the boundaries and guidelines for the use of force, the Just War tradition, thus became our recurring theme. Indeed, if we accept that the use of force can be legitimate in some circumstances, I can not imagine a moral framework that would look much different from Just War.

When I applied the Just War tradition earlier to the Global War on Terror and to military peace support interventions, the concept of reconciliation may have seemed quite distant. However, if Just War is to be applied in a flexible but holistic way, and not with the legalism that seems to have taken it over, decision-makers and commanders need to balance conflicting factors with the end state always in mind. The best do this already. And the post-war situation that should be in sight in almost any such conflict – however distant a goal it may seem – is a just, reconstructed society at ease with itself: a reconciled society. Christians should have much to offer in this, possessing as we do a faith that has reconciliation at its heart, however uncommon an assessment of the church this may be by outsiders. This is why the loss of ownership of the Just War tradition by the church is to be regretted. Our contribution as Christians to 'the problem of war' will be all the more effective if we can recognize our differences, admitting that others genuinely hold opposite views, but build on the common ground between us.

Peace-building and reconciliation

Having dealt with military intervention, we moved on to
recognize the limits of power, and to consider the many
non-military ways in which we can help those affected by
violent conflict to achieve and sustain comprehensive peace:
šālôm. We considered the whole range of activities that are
needed at three different levels of society, and related them
to phases of conflict by talking about conflict prevention,
conflict resolution and peace-building. Most importantly,
there is the need for the peace to be owned by those involved
in and affected by the violence. Without this ownership, the
chances of reconciliation in a society are very slim. Indeed,
resentment against those who have imposed a peace settlement may be added to the existing hatred of the enemy.

When I tell people in churches about the kind of work that
I and my colleagues at Concordis do, the reaction is often:
'Ah yes, you are doing reconciliation.' I sometimes let it go at
that, but things are in fact much more complex. Ultimately,
our goal must be reconciliation, but there are many different ways of approaching it, some of them not at all obvious.
When I described the work of Concordis International in
some detail earlier, I did not claim that it is a ministry of
reconciliation. Yet in a sense it is. The participants in our
consultations, working together on constitutional, water
or land issues, would perhaps not want to suggest they are
being reconciled. But by providing a safe space for enemies
to engage with one another, and by accompanying them on
a sort of journey towards consensus, we are approaching
reconciliation by the back door.

This also connects back to the several levels of society and
the wide range of peace-building activity described earlier.
There can be many kinds of involvement with a society shattered by violence, which contribute to reconciliation without

necessarily being called by that name. So sport, education, business, inter-religious dialogue, radio drama and any number of other activities can play a part. The details are hazy, but I remember being told about a brief morning radio spot on the BBC in Northern Ireland, where victims of conflict were given a few minutes simply to tell their stories. This was so powerful that drivers sometimes had to stop their cars to listen, often in tears.

Much of the work I have described already contributes in a similar way. It is of course then difficult to establish any proven link to the desired outcome: a reconciled society. However, as we observe the breadth and depth of different activities, operating in the same direction, interacting with one another and potentially reinforcing one another, we can see the connections between reconciliation and the various threads of this book.

A slow process with many hurdles

There are, of course, barriers to this progress. We have to recognize that a process of reconciliation does not achieve results overnight. Think of Germany and Britain. The reconciliation process since 1945, which we take for granted, has been a steady progress of cultural sharing, military partnership, economic cooperation and even intermarriages. My wife Ingrid is a product of one such marriage, the daughter of a young German woman and the British soldier who was billeted in her household as a member of the occupying Allied forces. She joined him in England in 1946 in bomb-scarred Liverpool, and as a better writer than I might have said, 'Reader, she married him.' But even today, if you listen to the kind of things English football fans say about Germans at an international match, you could be forgiven for thinking that the process of reconciliation still has not been completed after over sixty years. An example of how quickly reconciliation can be destroyed is former Yugoslavia. In Bosnia and Croatia, many intermarriages had taken place, but neighbours and even families were torn apart by the cynical politicization of ethnic differences as the republic slowly disintegrated.

Relationships are quickly destroyed, but take time to rebuild. In such an environment we need to be aware of the power of symbol and ritual, mentioned briefly in the previous chapter. Jesus commissioned Peter three times, connecting with his threefold denial. If we are looking at the level of society and not just at individuals, then we need to recognize the power of stories and language as transmitted by the media: by radio, television, newspapers and the Internet. This can be true, both in a negative sense, through insults, intended or not, and in a positive sense through acknowledgment of victims and by building cooperation. Perhaps the place where that impact is felt most deeply and lasts longest is among children and young people. So the images transmitted through education, including especially the way we teach history, are crucial. It is no accident that Musalaha, which we encountered earlier, focuses on the young, including children.

Health warnings

As I look back on what I have written, I am conscious of the need for three caveats or 'health warnings'. It is possible that some of the work I have been discussing could be accused of a form of 'peace-building imperialism', supposedly acting on the assumption that the third-party Westerners know best and are there in effect to impose solutions on those in a less 'enlightened' conflictual society. I hope that the broad sweep of what I have said will show that this is not the case. Our friends at the British organizations Conciliation Resources,

International Alert and particularly Peace Direct play an important role as they concentrate on building the capacity of local peace-building and civil society organizations. There are major issues of effectiveness, transparency and partisanship involving some such local organizations, but the principle of indigenous ownership of peace processes, as I have repeatedly emphasized, is crucial. We at Concordis aim to achieve such local ownership by working with a broad and inclusive group from the society involved.

The second health warning is related to the first. There is a danger that, by trying to analyse how peacemakers might go about their business, I may imply a form of instrumentalism, an idea that this or that technique, method or strategy will lead to this or that outcome or behaviour from the objects of our attentions, those who are fighting one another. But these are not objects, they are human beings, loved by God, and the danger is that we lose sight of the emotional and the spiritual if we become too analytical. This is not an approach I am describing or suggesting. We must beware of techniques and methods that we 'apply' to others. Rather, if we are given the privilege of playing a part in a reconciliation process, our strategy should be one of prayer, patience and dependence on God.

The third health warning relates to the limitations of this book, and it came to my mind when I heard news reports of the hijacking of an oil tanker by Somali pirates. This book focuses on how we can best serve those embroiled in civil wars. The question of how international lawlessness and piracy should be dealt with is a different one, another aspect of our response to violent conflict. It is one of the many facets of armed conflict that I could not hope to cover in the space available in this book. Suffice it to say that cases like Somali piracy represent one area that would make it very difficult for me to embrace pacifism.

How can we help?

As we've seen, we often steer clear of involving ourselves in the complexities of international problems. We feel that there is nothing that we can do, or we simply do not understand the issues. I hope that some of the contents of the preceding chapters will have helped a little to deal with the latter problem. But is there anything the individual Christian can really contribute?

Certainly, better understanding of the issues will help, whatever our situation. The motto of international development, 'Do no harm', is especially applicable in conflict situations. We have seen how development aid can become a war resource, how misdirected advocacy can lead to a waste of resources, or worse, how well-meaning 'peace missions' can put others' lives at risk, and how badly conceived military operations can lead to unexpected violent reactions. Sometimes the right thing to do is nothing.

Yet this is not always the case. Often, thoughtful and focused action can prevent or resolve conflict and save lives. This sounds too simple, and it is, of course. It is very rare that any individual action genuinely brings sustained peace. A rapid response to an urgent need, particularly by well-trained and well-led military forces, can impose stability, provide a breathing space and prevent a situation from deteriorating further. However, much more likely is that a range of actions by those intimately involved in the conflict, supported by outsiders, will slowly and progressively work towards or sustain long-term peace. This is so, whether or not violent conflict has actually broken out. Although the difficulties and political sensitivities of early warning are enormous – no state wants to be branded a 'basket case' – and the outcomes of early action are very uncertain, the potential 'return on investment' from preventive action is immense.

So, against this background, what can the individual Christian or a church congregation contribute?

We are not necessarily as helpless as we may feel. Even if we do not find ourselves in a profession that is directly relevant, most of us live in democracies of one kind or another. We are all voters and we have a voice. Properly informed, and not necessarily accepting all that we are told in the media, taking a balanced and thoughtful view, we can make our voice heard. There is a danger here. The information we receive through the media may be incomplete, biased or inaccurate. An emotional response may prevail. So we need actively to seek out the right information and, with benefit of the Internet, this is no longer difficult or expensive. There is a great deal of misleading, uncorroborated and even false information on the web, of course. The key is to find reliable sources.[1]

If, however, we are working in a field that plays a role in international politics or security issues, we can contribute much more directly. Or as we start out on a career or an educational path, maybe the skills and aptitudes with which we have been blessed, and perhaps a more direct calling, are leading us in such a direction. There are dangers here too. Working in an organization like the civil service or as a diplomat, we are not necessarily at liberty to make our own independent decisions, and this can be stifling. Sailors, soldiers and airmen, too, give up certain freedoms when they sign up, for they must obey lawful orders and can not express themselves politically. Yet if we believe that we have been put in that position for some purpose, then we can in a sense remain relaxed about this loss of personal freedom. We may be in positions where we can inform colleagues and influence policy, contributing to better decision-making.

Alternatively, we may be able to have an impact through our work in the media or political research, in development aid, or in business. In any of these situations, we will be able to deploy our improved understanding of conflict. Some of us may be called to become directly involved in international peacemaking. It is not a large field. Regrettably, resources are not available to finance large organizations. So there are few openings and this is not a career field for those who want to earn large salaries. At Concordis, for example, we employ a very small core staff; we need to keep costs within the funds we are able to raise. We are able to take a very limited number of volunteer interns to increase our capacity, but the day-to-day uncertainties we work with mean that we have to be careful not to promise volunteers the interesting and rewarding work they have a right to expect.

Each of us has many identities in various different contexts – family, work, church, community, nation – and it is not only as a citizen or in our work that we can make a difference.

Some may feel so strongly about peace that they will campaign against particular political policies, and the freedom to do this is an aspect of an open and relatively free society. We should cherish it. I would just plead for recognition that others may genuinely hold different views, that some may be already working towards sustainable peace in different ways, and that a combative rather than a cooperative approach may turn out to disrupt valuable work and in the end prove counter-productive.

Even if we are not in a position to get involved directly or moved to act politically, we still have rich resources that we can deploy in the cause of sustained peace. As churches or individuals, we can pray for the organizations that are working at different levels in this area. I have mentioned a few: Musalaha, Concordis International and Flame International are among them. We have financial resources, too, be they large or small, and these organizations need concrete support. Often, they find it more difficult to raise funds than do relief organizations, because they are not directly and visibly relieving suffering but trying to deal with some of its causes. However thoughtful we may believe ourselves to be, we are all susceptible to images that tug at our emotional heartstrings; we would be inhuman if that were not so.

Nearly six years have passed since we walked through the frozen streets of Kabul. I vividly remember taking turns in going to the unheated hut our guest house called its 'business centre' to draft funding proposals, each of us lasting about half an hour before we had to return to the wood stove to warm up our typing fingers. Today, much of the focus of our efforts is still on raising funds. Opportunities have arisen to work in different areas, where it has seemed that the 'Concordis model' of cooperative, patient, pragmatic peace-building could play a role. Often, we have been unable to take up the challenge, even though the amounts of money involved are tiny compared with the millions spent on peace-keeping and post-conflict reconstruction.

Despite the economic woes currently faced by the developed world, many readers of this book probably live in relative affluence. This raises questions of justice and compassion, of course, and there are many working to redress these balances. Violent conflict is one of the threats to the precarious existence of those who live in much worse conditions than us, and each of us has the opportunity to make a contribution, small or large, to dealing with this particular problem in our world.

We might recall the words of Jeremiah:

This is what the LORD says:
  'Let not the wise man boast of his wisdom
    or the strong man boast of his strength
    or the rich man boast of his riches,

but let him who boasts boast about this:
    that he understands and knows me,
  that I am the LORD, who exercises kindness,
    justice and righteousness on earth,
      for in these I delight,'
                  declares the LORD.[2]

Most of us probably react to this by thinking, 'We shouldn't boast at all.' Even the idea of boasting about our knowledge of God conjures images of hubris and pride. But the sting in this (admittedly selective) extract is in the tail. If we claim we know and understand God, then what we should know about him is his delight in kindness, justice and righteousness. Here there are echoes of Psalm 85:10, which we have seen earlier in this book. There peace, righteousness (or justice), truth and mercy meet together. They kiss.

Jeremiah does not mention peace, but the interconnections between these four aspects of God's character are scattered throughout the Bible. We may think ourselves wise, or strong, or rich, or knowledgeable about God. But it seems to me that the wisdom we may have gained through any privileged education, the relative riches we undoubtedly possess, and the power and strength we think we can wield to protect our way of life are of little value unless we apply them in line with what God delights in.

Being effective

Many of my predecessors who have delivered the London Lectures over the years have been distinguished scholars, and I make no claim to be one of them. What I had to say in my four lectures, developed into this book, has very definitely been the practitioner's view, an attempt to share knowledge gleaned over some years of working in this complex, difficult and sometimes confused field. Much of what I have said and written has come from what would be called secular sources, from the experts who have studied conflict and how it might be resolved or transformed without violence. Some of these experts are Christian, but a good number are not, and, where I have seen value in the ideas, I have brought them into the lectures and the book.

By examining the subject through a Christian lens, I have probably not done justice to other traditions. We should not, for example, imagine that other religions and traditions ignore the need for reconciliation. The Muslim tradition of *sulha* (mediation) is an approach that a more comprehensive examination would have described.

However, I have done my best to show the biblical principles that may lie behind these insights, even when the experts do not recognize them. I have gone back several times to the verses from Psalm 85 that speak about the complex relationships between peace, justice and mercy, and about God's sovereign role in the difficult issues we have been considering here. We need to bear these words in mind when we think about what makes for effectiveness in peacemaking.

It seems to me that in order to be effective, peacemaking needs to be owned by the most important people involved, namely those who are involved in or affected by the violence: *all* of them. Peacemaking also needs to be comprehensive, in several senses. In terms of time, it is too late to be dealing with a problem when the crisis has already erupted; responses are likely to be rushed, inadequate and wasteful. And peacemaking has to continue long after the bullets stop flying. In terms of levels of society, work needs to go on at the top political level, at the community level and at the important mid-level. And in terms of activity, there is a whole range of work that needs to be done. No one entity, even the most powerful, can do all of this, because no one entity has the knowledge, the commitment or the necessary weakness to fulfil some of the roles. Many hands rowing in the same direction, probably for a long time, will have a chance of getting the boat to its destination.

Many hands rowing in the same direction, probably for a long time, will have a chance of getting the boat to its destination.

In a sense, none of this is particularly controversial or particularly Christian. It is reasonably well understood. Yet we do not often seem to manage to get it right. I would suggest that Christians have an important role to play, in cooperation with others. And the reason is that believers at least *ought* to have the confidence in God, the faith, the hope to be able to continue in the face of disappointment and setback, as we trust in 'him who is able to do immeasurably more than all we ask or imagine'.[3]

BIBLIOGRAPHY

Ashdown, Paddy (2007), *Swords and Ploughshares: Bringing Peace to the 21st Century*, London: Weidenfeld & Nicolson.

Assefa, Hizkias, 'The Meaning of Reconciliation', www.gppac.net/documents/pbp/part1/2_reconc.htm

Azar, Edward E., Jureidini, Paul and McLaurin, Ronald (1978), 'Protracted Social Conflict; Theory and Practice in the Middle East', *Journal of Palestine Studies 8*, no. 1: 41–60.

Bainton, Roland H. (1946), 'The Early Church and War', *The Harvard Theological Review 39*, no. 3: 189–212.

Barclay, Oliver R. (1984), *Pacifism and War: When Christians Disagree*, Leicester: Inter-Varsity Press.

Bonhoeffer, Dietrich (1953), *Letters and Papers from Prison*, London: Collins Fontana Books.

Brickhill, Jeremy (2007), 'Protecting Civilians through Peace Agreements: Challenges and Lessons of the Darfur Peace Agreement', Pretoria: Institute for Security Studies.

Burton, John W. (1987), *Resolving Deep-Rooted Conflict: A Handbook*, Lanham, MD: University Press of America.

Clark, Ian. (1997), *Globalization and Fragmentation: International Relations in the Twentieth Century*, Oxford: Oxford University Press.

Cole, Darrell. (2002), *When God Says War Is Right: The Christian's Perspective on When and How to Fight*, 1st edn Colorado Springs, CO: Waterbrook Press.

Cox, Brian, and Philpott, Daniel (2003), 'Faith-Based Diplomacy: An Ancient Idea Newly Emergent', *Brandywine Review of Faith and International Affairs*, no. Fall 2003.

Daly, M. W. (2007), *Darfur's Sorrow: A History of Destruction and Genocide*, New York: Cambridge University Press.

Elshtain, Jean Bethke (2008), *Sovereignty: God, State, and Self*, New York: Basic Books.

Flint, Julie, and De Waal, Alexander (2008), *Darfur: A New History of a Long War*, London: Zed.

Franck, Thomas M., and Rodley, Nigel S. (1973), 'After Bangladesh: The Law of Humanitarian Intervention by Military Force', *American Journal of International Law 67*, no. 2: 275–305.

Guthrie, Charles, and Quinlan, Michael (2007), *Just War: The Just War Tradition: Ethics in Modern Warfare*, London: Bloomsbury.

Helgeland, John (1974), 'Christians and the Roman Army A.D. 173–337', *Church History 43*, no. 2: 149–200.

Kaldor, Mary (2006), *New and Old Wars: Organized Violence in a Global Era*, Cambridge: Polity Press.

Kempster, Tony (2008), 'The Ethics of Pacifism and Just War in an Age of Terrorist Violence', *Modern Believing* 49, no. 2.

Lederach, John Paul (1997), *Building Peace: Sustainable Reconciliation in Divided Societies*, Washington, DC: United States Institute of Peace Press.

Lewis, C. S. (2002), *The Problem of Pain*, C. S. Lewis Signature Classics, London: Fount.

Lewis, C. S., and Walmsley, Lesley (2000), C. S. Lewis: *Essay Collection and Other Short Pieces*, London: HarperCollins.

Lund, Michael S. (1995), 'Underrating Preventive Diplomacy', *Foreign Affairs* 74, no. 4: 160–63.

Nye, Joseph S. (2004), 'The Decline of America's Soft Power', *Foreign Affairs*.

Pearse, Meic. (2007), *The Gods of War: Is Religion the Primary Cause of Violent Conflict?*, Downers Grove, IL; Nottingham: Inter-Varsity Press.

Princen, Thomas (1992), *Intermediaries in International Conflict*, Princeton, NJ; Oxford: Princeton University Press.

Ramachandra, Vinoth (2008), *Subverting Global Myths: Theology and the Public Issues Facing Our World*, London: SPCK.

Ramsbotham, Oliver, Miall, Hugh and Woodhouse, Tom, eds. (2005), *Contemporary Conflict Resolution: The Prevention, Management and Transformation of Deadly Conflicts*, Cambridge: Polity Press.

Reed, Charles, and Ryall, David, eds. (2007), *The Price of Peace: Just War in the Twenty-First Century*, Cambridge: Cambridge University Press.

Schluter, Michael, and Ashcroft, John (2005), *Jubilee Manifesto: A Framework, Agenda and Strategy for Christian Social Reform*, Nottingham: Inter-Varsity Press.

Schluter, Michael, and Lee, David J. (1993), *The R Factor*, London: Hodder & Stoughton.

Schreiter, Robert J. (1998), *The Ministry of Reconciliation: Spirituality and Strategies*, Maryknoll, New York: Orbis Books.

Simmons, Mark, and Dixon, Peter, eds. (2006), *Peace by Piece: Addressing Sudan's Conflicts*, edited by Aaron Griffiths, vol. 18, Accord, London: Conciliation Resources.

Skillen, James W. (2005), *With or Against the World? America's Role Among the Nations*, Lanham, MD: Rowman & Littlefield Publishers.

Sorabji, Richard, and Rodin, David, eds. (2006), *The Ethics of War: Shared Problems in Different Traditions*, Aldershot: Ashgate.

Stephan, Maria J, and Chenoweth, Erica, 'Why Civil Resistance Works: The Strategic Logic of Nonviolent Conflict', *International Security* 33, no. 1: 7–44.

Stott, John R.W. (1999), *Issues Facing Christians Today*, 3rd edn, London: Marshall Pickering.

Stowell, Ellery C. (1939), 'Humanitarian Intervention', *American Journal of International Law* 33, no. 4: 733–36.

Walzer, Michael (2000), *Just and Unjust Wars: A Moral Argument with Historical Illustrations*, 3rd edn, New York: Basic Books.

Weyeneth, Robert R. (2001), 'The Power of Apology and the Process of Historical Reconciliation', *The Public Historian* 23, no. 3: 9–38.

Yoder, John Howard (1994), *The Politics of Jesus: Vicit Agnus Noster ('Our Lamb Has Conquered')*, 2nd edn, Carlisle, UK, and Grand Rapids, Michigan: Paternoster and Eerdmans.

Zartman, I. William. (2005), *Cowardly Lions: Missed Opportunities to Prevent Deadly Conflict and State Collapse*, Boulder, CO: Lynne Rienner.

GLOSSARY

asymmetric warfare	Warfare between opponents of dissimilar power, often characterized by unconventional means of warfare used by the weaker party.
CNN effect	The impact on political and military decision-making caused by public access to real-time news reporting of conflict and crisis situations.
communitarianism	A social philosophy that, over against individualism, emphasizes the needs, rights and perspectives of communities.
CPA	Comprehensive Peace Agreement signed in January 2005 between the government of Sudan and the (Southern Sudanese) Sudan People's Liberation Army. The agreement allowed for a vote by southerners on secession after 6½ years, i.e. in 2011.
DDR	The process of disarmament, demobilization and reintegration of former combatants following the cessation of armed conflict. Reintegration may include enrolling of fighters in the state's armed forces or providing them with civilian employment or other means of livelihood.
DPA	Darfur Peace Agreement signed in May 2006 by the government of Sudan and the Sudan Liberation Army (Minni Minawi).
Enlightenment	A period of philosophical change, centred on the eighteenth century and characterized by the desire for human affairs to be guided by rationality rather than by religious faith. The period is seen by many as laying the foundations of modern Western political and intellectual culture.

interdict	To disrupt enemy force movements, reinforcements and supplies on their way to the battlefield.
jus ad bellum	Just War 'rules' about going to war: just cause; war the only reasonable option; right intention; legitimate authority; proportionality; reasonable probability of success.
jus in bello	Just War 'rules' about behaviour during war: discrimination between combatants and non-combatants; proportionality.
jus post bellum	Just War 'rules' about post-war peace and stability.
military covenant	The implicit agreement between the military and the state or community it serves, whereby the latter is expected to provide both tangible and moral support for the former.
militia	A military force raised from the community and composed of ordinary citizens.
natural law	Universally valid law whose content is implicit in nature.
NGO	Non-governmental organization.
peace support operations	Military operations designed to impose or maintain peace and stability in a conflictual situation.
positive law	Law created by proper authority for a political community.
Responsibility to Protect	The principle, developed in 2001 under Canadian government sponsorship and accepted by the United Nations in 2005, that a state has a responsibility for the human rights and security of its citizens. By implication, a state that is seen to fail in this responsibility faces the threat of outside intervention.
soft power	The ability to achieve political goals through non-coercive means, using 'weapons' such as culture, attractiveness, values and economic assistance.

NOTES

1. War in the twenty-first century

1. C. S. Lewis, *The Problem of Pain*, C.S. Lewis Signature Classics (London: Fount, 2002).
2. Oliver Ramsbotham, Hugh Miall, and Tom Woodhouse, eds., *Contemporary Conflict Resolution: The Prevention, Management and Transformation of Deadly Conflicts* (Cambridge: Polity Press, 2005).
3. Ian Clark, *Globalization and Fragmentation: International Relations in the Twentieth Century* (Oxford: Oxford University Press, 1997).
4. Mary Kaldor, *New and Old Wars: Organized Violence in a Global Era* (Cambridge: Polity Press, 2006).
5. See Edward E. Azar, Paul Jureidini, and Ronald McLaurin, 'Protracted Social Conflict; Theory and Practice in the Middle East', *Journal of Palestine Studies* 8, no. 1 (1978).
6. See John W. Burton, *Resolving Deep-Rooted Conflict: A Handbook* (Lanham, MD: University Press of America, 1987).
7. James 4:1–2.
8. See Meic Pearse, *The Gods of War: Is Religion the Primary Cause of Violent Conflict?* (Downers Grove, IL; Nottingham: Inter-Varsity Press, 2007).
9. Vinoth Ramachandra, *Subverting Global Myths: Theology and the Public Issues Facing Our World* (London: SPCK, 2008), pp. 56–90.

2. The Christian and war

1. Quoted by permission of The Random House Group.
2. John 15:13.
3. For example, see Oliver R. Barclay, *Pacifism and War: When Christians Disagree* (Leicester: Inter-Varsity Press, 1984). Also Charles Guthrie and Michael Quinlan, *Just War: The Just War Tradition: Ethics in Modern Warfare* (London: Bloomsbury, 2007).
4. Charles Reed and David Ryall, eds., *The Price of Peace: Just War in the Twenty-First Century* (Cambridge: Cambridge University Press, 2007).
5. Tony Kempster, 'The Ethics of Pacifism and Just War in an Age of Terrorist Violence', *Modern Believing* 49, no. 2 (2008).
6. Acts 7:59; 1 Corinthians 4:9–13.
7. Mark 12:14–17.
8. Luke 3:14; 7:1–10.
9. See Roland H. Bainton, 'The Early Church and War', *The Harvard Theological Review* 39, no. 3 (1946). See also John Helgeland, 'Christians and the Roman Army A.D. 173–337', *Church History* 43, no. 2 (1974).
10. 1 Corinthians 7:17–24.
11. Several writers have commented on the conflation of religion and state in the USA, encapsulated in the depth of meaning and emotion carried in the phrase

'God bless America', even for secular citizens. See for example James W. Skillen, *With or Against the World?: America's Role Among the Nations* (Lanham, MD: Rowman & Littlefield Publishers, 2005).

12. Cited in Darrell Cole, *When God Says War Is Right: The Christian's Perspective on When and How to Fight*, 1st edn (Colorado Springs, CO: Waterbrook Press, 2002), pp. 16–17.

13. Augustine, letter to Boniface, *Epist.* 189, 6 and 209, 2.

14. Michael Walzer, *Just and Unjust Wars: A Moral Argument with Historical Illustrations*, 3rd edn (New York: Basic Books, 2000).

15. For a comparison of ethical approaches to warfare in different religious traditions, see Richard Sorabji and David Rodin, eds., *The Ethics of War: Shared Problems in Different Traditions* (Aldershot: Ashgate, 2006).

16. Suggested by Darrell Cole in Cole, *When God Says War Is Right: The Christian's Perspective on When and How to Fight.*

17. Luke 14:31–32.

18. Isaiah 2:4.

19. 2 Chronicles 19:6–7; Deuteronomy 16:18–20; Proverbs 17:15; Proverbs 31:8–9.

20. Romans 13:1–7.

21. Romans 12:19.

22. 'Why I am not a Pacifist', in C. S. Lewis and Lesley Walmsley, *C.S. Lewis: Essay Collection and Other Short Pieces* (London: HarperCollins, 2000), p. 291.

23. For example, see Barclay, *Pacifism and War*. Also, John Stott deals thoughtfully with this issue in Stott, John R. W. *Issues Facing Christians Today*, 3rd edn London: Marshall Pickering, 1999.

3. Just War on Terror

1. Archived at http://georgewbush-whitehouse.archives.gov/nsc/nss/2002/index.html

2. Skillen, *With or Against the World?: America's Role Among the Nations.*

4. Intervening in conflict – the military way

1. Report of the Panel on United Nations Peace Operations, August 2000, known as the 'Brahimi Report' after the Panel Chairman, available at www.un.org/peace/reports/peace_operations

2. See Paddy Ashdown, *Swords and Ploughshares: Bringing Peace to the 21st Century* (London: Weidenfeld & Nicolson, 2007).

3. Michael Schluter and John Ashcroft, *Jubilee Manifesto: A Framework, Agenda and Strategy for Christian Social Reform* (Nottingham: Inter-Varsity Press, 2005), pp. 267–269.

4. St Augustine of Hippo, *City of God Book IV Ch 4.*

5. The report of the International Commission on Intervention and State Sovereignty, which was substantially accepted by the United Nations General Assembly in September 2005, can be found at www.iciss.ca/menu-en.asp

6. Thomas More, *Utopia* (1516), ed. George M. Logan and Robert M. Adams (Cambridge: Cambridge University Press, 1989), pp. 87–88.

7. E.g. Romans 13:1–7; 1 Peter 2:13–14; Matthew 9:36; Matthew 25:44–45.

8. Thomas M. Franck and Nigel S. Rodley, 'After Bangladesh: The Law of Humanitarian Intervention by Military Force', *American Journal of International Law* 67, no. 2 (1973).

9. Ellery C. Stowell, 'Humanitarian Intervention', *American Journal of International Law* 33, no. 4 (1939).

10. Jean Bethke Elshtain, *Sovereignty: God, State, and Self* (New York: Basic Books, 2008).

11. Gareth Evans is a former Foreign Minister of Australia who served as co-chair of the International Commission on Intervention and State Sovereignty in 2000–2001 and as CEO of International Crisis Group until 2009.

12. Luke 10:29–37.

5. Power and weakness

1. Interview with then Major Chris Keeble in video 'Command and the Christian Faith', published by the Armed Forces Christian Union.
2. Matthew 8:5–13.
3. Joseph S. Nye, 'The Decline of America's Soft Power', *Foreign Affairs* (2004). Also a lecture given at Princeton University on 8 May 2002.
4. Matthew 5:39.
5. John Howard Yoder, *The Politics of Jesus: Vicit Agnus Noster ('Our Lamb Has Conquered')*, 2nd edn (Carlisle, UK, and Grand Rapids, Michigan: Paternoster and Eerdmans, 1994).
6. Maria J. Stephan and Erica Chenoweth, 'Why Civil Resistance Works: The Strategic Logic of Nonviolent Conflict', *International Security* 33, no. 1.
7. Psalm 20:7; Isaiah 31:1.
8. Dietrich Bonhoeffer, *Letters and Papers from Prison* (London: Collins Fontana Books, 1953), p. 142.
9. For most of its length, the separation barrier is constructed as a series of fence structures up to fifty metres across, but in the urban areas like Jerusalem it consists of a high concrete wall.
10. 2 Corinthians 12:9–10.
11. 1 Corinthians 1:18–31.

6. Intervening in armed conflict – the non-military way

1. Michael S. Lund, 'Underrating Preventive Diplomacy', *Foreign Affairs* 74, no. 4 (1995).
2. I. William Zartman, *Cowardly Lions: Missed Opportunities to Prevent Deadly Conflict and State Collapse* (Boulder, CO: Lynne Rienner, 2005).
3. 2 Peter 3:8.
4. In Mark Simmons and Peter Dixon, eds., *Peace by Piece: Addressing Sudan's Conflicts*, vol. 18, Accord (London: Conciliation Resources, 2006).
5. Thomas Princen, *Intermediaries in International Conflict* (Princeton, NJ; Oxford: Princeton University Press, 1992).
6. Jeremy Ive, *Peacebuilding from a Biblical Perspective* (2003), available at www.jubilee-centre.org
7. John Paul Lederach, *Building Peace: Sustainable Reconciliation in Divided Societies* (Washington, DC: United States Institute of Peace Press, 1997).
8. Jeremy Brickhill, 'Protecting Civilians through Peace Agreements: Challenges and Lessons of the Darfur Peace Agreement', (Pretoria: Institute for Security Studies, 2007).

7. Relational peace-building

1. A helpful history of Darfur is M.W. Daly, *Darfur's Sorrow: A History of Destruction and Genocide* (New York: Cambridge University Press, 2007). A book on the current war is Julie Flint and Alexander De Waal, *Darfur: A New History of a Long War* (London: Zed, 2008).
2. Michael Schluter and colleagues have written extensively on relational matters. See Michael Schluter and David J. Lee, *The R Factor* (London: Hodder & Stoughton, 1993), Schluter and Ashcroft, *Jubilee Manifesto: A Framework, Agenda and Strategy for Christian Social Reform*.
3. See www.relationshipsfoundation.org and www.jubilee-centre.org.

8. Be reconciled

1. See www.musalaha.org
2. Hizkias Assefa, 'The Meaning of Reconciliation', www.gppac.net/documents/pbp/part1/2_reconc.htm
3. New King James Version.

4. Robert J Schreiter, *The Ministry of Reconciliation: Spirituality and Strategies* (Maryknoll, NY: Orbis Books, 1998), p. 4.

5. Brian Cox and Daniel Philpott, 'Faith-Based Diplomacy: An Ancient Idea Newly Emergent', *Brandywine Review of Faith and International Affairs*, no. Fall 2003 (2003): 35.

6. The brief paper that resulted from the consultation is available at www.concordis-international.org

7. Matthew 6:15.

8. Robert R. Weyeneth, 'The Power of Apology and the Process of Historical Reconciliation', *The Public Historian* 23, no. 3 (2001).

9. Schreiter, *The Ministry of Reconciliation: Spirituality and Strategies*.

10. 2 Corinthians 5:17–18.

11. Luke 24:13–35.

12. Depicted in two striking paintings by Caravaggio, one located in the National Gallery, London, the other in the Pinacoteca di Brera, Milan.

13. John 21:1–17.

9. Effective Christian engagement in twenty-first-century conflict

1. Useful sources include: www.crisisweb.org, which provides detailed reports and updates on conflict situations, although you should make up your own mind whether their recommendations are valid; http://news.bbc.co.uk, which is a source not only of up-to-date news reports, but also of in-depth background information; www.economist.com, with a vast range of political information and opinion; www.humansecuritygateway.info and www.eldis.org, which are rich resources providing links to academic research papers, respectively on human security and on a wider range of development issues.

2. Jeremiah 9:23–24.

3. Ephesians 3:20.